INTRODUCTION

This book is aimed at those coaches and teachers who are involved in teaching various 'technical models' associated with track and field athletics. It is my inter of these pages represents a reservoir of introductory practices, which I hope y more advanced texts, and by gaining greater experience of practical coaching.

I feel most strongly that the beginner athlete must be well taught, with teachers and coaches committed to ensuring that the various 'technical models' are stabilised *before* moving on to competition or advanced training.

The years 8 – 11 for girls and 8 – 13 for boys have been referred to as the 'skill-hungry years'. Hopefully, teachers and coaches will concentrate on these age groups, and use their ingenuity and inventiveness to apply the information in this booklet to the advantage of their young charges.

Frank W. Dick, O.B.E.
Director of Coaching, B.A.F.

INDEX

© BRITISH ATHLETIC FEDERATION
225A Bristol Road, Edgbaston, Birmingham B5 7UB

ATHLETICS COACH

The Coaching Journal of the B.A.F.

Published: March, June, September, December

Details from: Malcolm Arnold
56 Rolls Avenue, Penpedairheol, Hengoed, Mid Glamorgan CF8 8HQ

THROWS

Development of throwing events is best thought of as growing from a 'common root' movement. Certainly this is the case with Javelin, Shot and Discus, while the Hammer, although resting on similar principles, should be introduced from a slightly different approach.

The 'common root' idea is based on the fact that, at their most fundamental level, the Shot, Discus and Javelin involve (in the right handed thrower), the following action sequences:-

1 Rotation of the right hip over a bent right knee, towards the direction of the throw.

2 Transfer of weight from the right foot forward onto the left foot – by extending the right ankle/knee.

3 Extension of the left ankle/knee/hip.

In other words, the right lower limb gives the body *forward* (horizontal) movement via *rotation* and *extension*; the left lower limb gives the body *upward* (vertical) movement via extension.

By 'the body', I mean the strong pillar of the hip/spine complex, which, in rotating forward *adds* to the movement started by the right lower limb.

The totality of this movement is finally transferred to the shoulder/arm complex, which, in turn, adds its very fast contribution to the release of the implement.

The contribution of right lower limb, hips/spine/ – and shoulders/arm provides the *release velocity* of the implement, while the left lower limb/hip – plus a 'lifting' left side, provides the *release angle* of the implement.

These 'common root' movements are so very important, that the athlete learning to throw discus, javelin or shot *must* be able to reproduce them if he is to proceed to the specifics of individual events.

A West German coach, SCHWANBECK, used the exercise illustrated in figure 1 to introduce shot, but it is my firm belief that this particular exercise, in capturing the fundamental features of the 'common root' movement, is ideal for the introduction of Shot, Javelin and Discus. (figures 2, 3 and 4)

fig. 1

fig. 2

fig. 3

fig. 4

The 'common root' practice should be commenced with the athlete attempting to have *both* feet pointing in the direction of the throw. This will help *ensure* that he moves the hips *before* the shoulders.

1

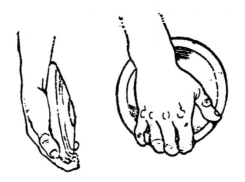

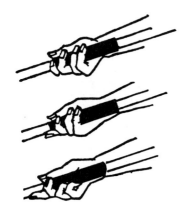

GETTING
TO
GRIPS
WITH THE
THROWS

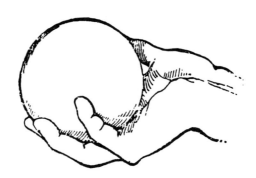

DISCUS

figure 5

The Basic Throw (standing)

Once the 'common root' movement has been learned, the athlete has a 'reference model' as it were, for the 'feel' of lower limb/trunk/upper limb movement training, and for the actions themselves. Discus may be readily developed from this model.

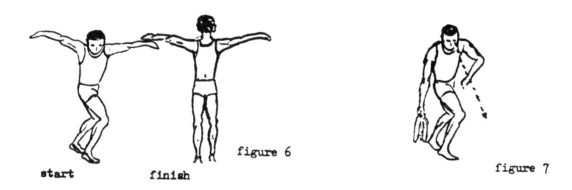

start   finish   figure 6   figure 7

To reinforce the basic model, the practice illustrated in figure 6 may be employed. The athlete is instructed to spin the right heel outwards – and stand up tall, facing 180° from his starting position. The right leg/hip is felt by the athlete to pull the trunk/shoulders towards the direction of 'throw'. Just as important, however, is the finishing position of extending the body upwards – hips raised, back straight, and shoulders square to the direction of 'throw'.

The next stage is to hold a towel in the right hand, with the left arm held away from the 'throw' ("Look at the time"). (figure 7). The weight is kept over the right foot as before, with the *right heel always off the ground,* i.e. the weight is on the ball of the foot – with the right hip pressing out towards the right of the 'throw'. The towel is then swung back and forward – (1 - 2 - 3), then on the final swing back, the right heel is spun outwards initiating the right leg/hip rotation. The right arm swings out with the force of the hip's pull, and the athlete finishes again 'standing tall' – shoulders square to the throw.

The final stage in the 'standing throw' is to go through this practice with a discus held in the end joints of the fingers, thumb pressed against the surface of the discus.

Emphasise:-

1 Weight back on the ball of the right foot; hip pressed out to right of throw; left arm wrapped across chest.

2 Spin-out of right heel – (*right knee bent*) – *fast* turn of right hip to front.

3 Extend the right knee/ankle – pulling trunk and shoulders through to the front.

4 Extend and brake with the left side.

There should be little problem with discus release. However, occasionally the discus may not come off the index finger but out of the back of the hand (i.e. off the little finger). Should this happen, check the point of release (shoulders square to the front, with the right arm an extension of the plane of the shoulders. If there still are problems – revert to rolling the discus along the ground!

The Turn

The purpose of the turn is to add to the *release velocity* of the discus. This is achieved by *horizontal movement across the circle in the direction of the throw* – and by *rotating* in doing so.

This complex movement is quite a feat of balance, and the athlete must learn from the very outset that he must balance over the *left* foot at the *rear* of the circle; and over the *right* foot when in the *throwing position* (i.e. the basic throw position already described).

Whatever the athlete does in his turn and movement across the circle, it *must* bring him to the basic throwing position *well balanced*. The whole feeling of balance starts from the back of the circle. If he is not balanced here, his chance of being balanced in the throwing position is considerably reduced.

figure 8

There are several ways of developing the turn. For example:-

1 (figure 8)
    (a) The athlete walks through the turn.
    (b) The athlete walks through the turn, emphasising balance on left foot – then on right.
    (c) As b, but with knees bent – and conscious movement into the basic throw.
    (d) Speed is gradually added.

    It is worth noting at this juncture that the right leg

    — is carried *low* and *long* into the middle of the circle
    — that the right foot begins its turn/spin as soon as the ball of the foot meets the middle of the circle
    — that the right knee is well bent in the middle of the circle
    — that the feeling throughout is of being balanced on the balls of the feet.

figure 9

2 (figure 9)

    The athlete begins the turn from the back of the circle by:-

    (a) Learning to pivot/spin on the spot, on the ball of the left foot – with left knee bent.
    (b) Keeping the right foot in contact with the circle, until the left has pointed towards the direction of the throw.

3 The athlete may 'hop' through the complete movement.

    Should the heel turn be used (figure 10) – then the athlete pivots on the heel rather than the ball of the left foot – *but then must transfer the weight onto the ball* to achieve the same balance position discussed above. If not, the left hip tends to 'sit', and the athlete has balance problems thereafter in the throw.

    Turning practices may be done with the right hand behind the back (figure 11); holding a towel in the right hand; using a sling ball (figure 12); carrying a short caber (figure 13) etc.

4

figure 10

Conditioning

Using the technical model of the discus throw, the coach should not find it difficult to devise special exercises for the development of the athlete's strength for the event. Figures 14 – 24 illustrate some such exercises.

fig. 11

fig. 12

fig. 13

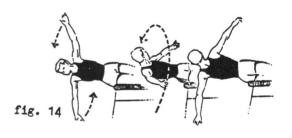

fig. 14

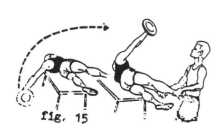

fig. 15

fig. 16

5

fig. 17

fig. 18

fig. 19

fig. 20

fig. 21

fig. 22

fig. 23

fig. 24

SHOT PUT

figure 25

The Basic Put (standing)

It is absolutely essential that the athlete has mastered the 'common root' exercise if he is to avoid the problems which are associated with right leg/hip action relative to the trunk/shoulder action in shot.

There are many ways of developing the basic put from this point. One method is as follows:-

figure 26

(a) Feet placed as per 'common root' exercise, holding shot to neck; bend right knee whilst taking the weight *back* over the right foot:

    Push the right hip forwards *fast* – with a driving action of the right leg:

    Lift the left hip by straightening the left knee and reaching high with the left shoulder:

    Push the right shoulder/arm/shot *upwards*.

    The finishing position is *very* similar, then, to that of discus.

    The shot is held by the length of the fingers – and is pressed into the neck (clean palm – dirty neck!). The final releasing of the shot is 'springing out' action of the fingers.

    At all times, the right elbow is held out – as an extension of the line of the shoulder.

    Much has been said of the braking or bracing action of the left side. I believe that this should take care of itself *if*

7

    i   the athlete lifts upwards with the left leg/hip/trunk/shoulder:

    ii the athlete always attempts to finish with *both shoulders high – and square to the direction of the throw.*

This applies both to shot, and to discus.

The shot should be only as heavy as allows the athlete to concentrate on the total technique. Thus, large stones, tennis balls filled with sand, 1kg – 4kg ball bearings, etc. are useful.

(b)   The athlete gradually turns the shoulders further away from the direction of put, when he takes his weight back over the right foot (figure 27).

Another method worth considering is that used by SCHWANBECK (figure 28).

figure 27

figure 28

Yet another was that devised by the late Alec Dalrymple.

(a)   The athlete puts *both* feet to the stop board (line) and puts using arm action only. He marks distance achieved.

(b)   The same process but with trunk twist.

(c)   As for b, but 'sitting' as he twists back, and standing up very fast as he 'unwinds'.

(d)   As for c, but with feet as per 'common root' exercise *except* that the right foot is turned out to approximately 90°.

    One advantage of this method is that the recorded distance amply illustrates for each athlete, the contribution of legs and trunk.

Movement into the Basic Put

The problem here is not simply to achieve movement across the circle, yet to arrive in the basic putting position, but how to ensure that the movement *adds* to the efficiency of the put.

There are two accepted techniques. The first is the 'shift', the other is the turn.

The Shift

There are many ways to approach this techique. I would suggest the following.

The athlete must move his position of shoulders parallel to hip; to hips at right angles to shoulders (figure 29).

(a)   I would suggest that the athlete practises 'jumping' his hips round, whilst keeping the shoulders in a constant position (twister!).

(b)   This may be developed by jumping backwards at the same time.

(c) Now the athlete should do the 'jumping' with the weight always on the right foot.

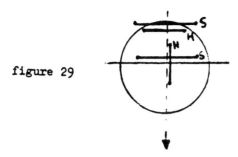

figure 29

(d) The next development is to attempt c, with the trunk kept low over the right leg.

This might be helped by *bending* the right leg – and allowing the hips to 'fall' towards the front of the circle, before snapping the hips round.

— If the shoulders are coming round early, the athlete should 'look at his watch' – and towards the rear of the circle.

— There is also a possible danger of the trunk lifting early – thus bringing the athlete's weight *between* the legs rather than over the right leg. The coach should develop practices to keep the trunk low, e.g. coach holding the shoulders down; coach holding athlete's left arm-shoulder; shifting under a cane, etc.

— The left leg action may be developed by practices such as that shown in figures 30 – 31.

figure 30

figure 31

The Turn

For this technique – the approach is similar to the discus turn.

Conditioning

Conditioning is always important in this event, and, on the basis of sound strength of legs/hips/trunk/shoulders/arms, specific exercises based on the technical model of the event should be developed by the coach. Some examples are illustrated in figures 32 – 37.

fig.32

fig.33

fig. 34

fig.35

fig.36

fig.37

JAVELIN

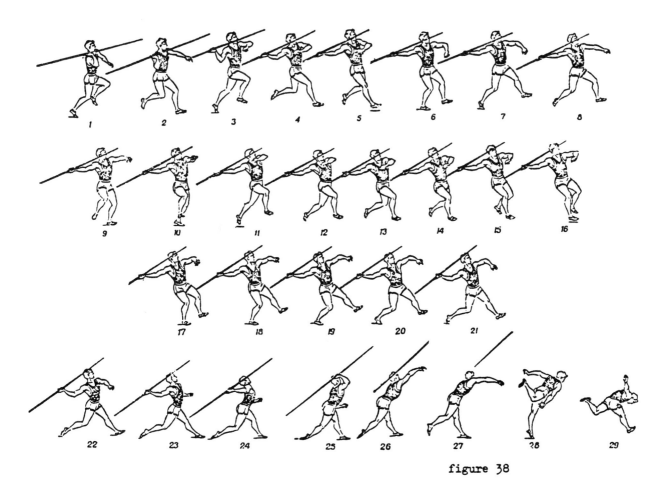

figure 38

The Basic Throw (standing)

The 'common root' exercise is very closely related to the basic javelin throw. Once the 'common root' exercise has been mastered, the athlete should attempt this movement, holding a small, heavy ball (figure 39). This could well be a tennis ball filled with sand, a stone, a 1kg ball bearing, a sling-ball, etc. *He must always finish the throw with the shoulders square to the direction of the throw, and with the sensation of lifting with the left side.* Hopefully, the arm action should be firmly understood by this time, but, if not, it is like a one-arm soccer throw-in, or like combing one's hair forward. The hand should be thought of as passing over the head – even although, in cine film, athletes are seen to be pulling the hand further out – towards the shoulder.

figure 39

Top athletes say that when they are throwing well, the right elbow comes *underneath* the javelin – but this feat of wrist/elbow/shoulder co-ordination and mobility may not be possible for the young thrower.

Next, the athlete should begin to emphasise the speed at which the right heel is 'spun' out, and the right hip pushed towards the front, above a *bent* knee.

The javelin should now replace the heavy ball. There are at least three accepted methods of holding the javelin, but I would recommend that which has the *middle finger* against the binding. This may be achieved quite simply, by gripping the javelin (a fistful!) on the tail side of the binding – then sliding the javelin through the 'grip' until the hand meets the binding.

The next stage is to step into the throw – i.e. step onto the left foot from the right (figures 40,41).

figure 40   figure 41

The Approach

The athlete should practice running forwards, while his shoulders are turned to the right. This may be done with or without a javelin – *but always on the heels.* This practice may be extended to a run + throw – first off 3 strides, then 4, then 5.

I do not believe that it is necessary to oblige an athlete to think of 'cross steps' or even to over-emphasise the 'withdrawal'. The running action with shoulders turned, and the athlete's own inclination towards a given stride for withdrawal should suffice at this stage.

The 'building-up' of the approach may best be achieved by adding strides in 2's or 4's (figure 42). The speed of approach should be that which the athlete can use to advantage.

figure 42

Directing the flight of the javelin is often a problem – and the athlete should learn how to 'feel' the javelin in order to guide it. Certainly, there should be a sensation of throwing *along the length of the javelin (figure 43).* Target throwing is worth including in training – along a line, at a circular target on the ground, etc.

Opening the shoulders is also a problem, and it may be useful to encourage the athlete to keep his left arm wrapped across his chest.

However, the greatest difficulty for the athlete will always be the fast movement of the right hip under and ahead of the shoulder. This must be well drilled – and I believe that this is best achieved by standing 1-step and 3-step throws.

figure 43

Always the athlete must be encouraged to run at the throw – this may reduce the possibility of slowing down on the last strides.

If the javelin is 'stalling' encourage the athlete to keep the 'nose' down – even although he is throwing upwards.

Conditioning

Conditioning is very important. Running and hurling must be included in training – and, on the basis of sound strength background of work on legs/hips/trunk/shoulders/arm, specific exercises, based on the technical model should be developed by the coach. Figures 44 – 55 are examples of such specific exercises.

12

fig.44

fig.45

fig.46

fig.47

fig.48

fig.49

fig.50

fig.51   c   b   a

fig.52

fig.53

fig.54

fig.55

14.

HAMMER

figure 56

The Basic Throw (standing)

The athlete should think of this action as one of lifting/heaving rather than of throwing (figure 57). The principles of lifting certainly apply here. i.e.

— back held stiff and vertical (a *strong* back).

— work done by legs, not back.

— arms simply attach the load (here – the hammer) to the shoulders/back.

This lifting action might first be introduced via a simple lift-throw (figure 57).

However, the lift is, in fact, from outside the right foot – diagonally across the body – to be released high over the left shoulder (figure 58).

figure 57   figure 58

This being the case, we have once again the principle of a movement initiated and given a *'throw direction' and release velocity by the right leg/hip* – and given *height and release angle by the left side.*

Life is actually quite difficult for the thrower if the throw is performed without a preliminary 'swing'. So quite early in the learning situation, the athlete should be encouraged to learn the swings.

The swings should be developed as follows:-

(a)   Using something like a wooden baton or a brush, the athlete is introduced to the idea of shifting the hip weight from one leg to the other – countering and anticipating the 'pull' of the baton/brush (figure 59).

14

figure 59

(b)   The low-high point should come quite naturally, but, for reference, the low point is beyond the right foot (general area), while the high point is over the left shoulder.

(c)   Arms should always be *long* – with back vertical, and knees bent.

(d)   As the baton/brush passes upwards from the left foot, the athlete moves the hands in a motion that resembles brushing the sweat from his forehead with the back of his right hand. The body is, then, countering a wide sweep of the baton/brush head.

(e)   The baton/brush should now be replaced by a short-handle hammer (or similar device, e.g. sand sack + rope and handle, medicine ball in a string bag, chain-bunch + handle, etc.) (figure 60).

figure 60

(f)   The athlete now performs the swing + a throw.

– Always finish with shoulders high and weight on *both* feet.

The next stage is to develop the turn. There seems little escape from very direct teaching method here. The turn is on the ball of the right foot, and on the heel of the left. The weight passes along the outside of the left foot (right toe still in contact). When the weight reaches the ball of the left small toe (!) the right knee is picked up bent and fast – keeping close to the left knee. The right leg action is like the pumping action of operating a stirrup pump (figure 61). The athlete should practise holding nothing in his hand, then with a baton/brush (figure 62), then with a short hammer (figure 63). The turn should be practised along a line to check the direction of progress and the alignment of the feet after each turn (figure 64).

fig.61

fig.62

The progression should be 2 swings – 1 turn – throw – checking the *long arm*; *vertical back*; *sitting posture of the hips*; *pumping action of the right knee*; *the turning actions of the body always preceding the ball of the hammer*.

Gradually 2, then 3 turns are used.

The regular hammer length and weight should be gradually approached – with great care being taken to ensure that long arms; vertical back, etc. are always a feature of the throw.

15

fig.63

fig.64

Conditioning

Strength is a *very* important feature in conditioning of the athlete for this event. Legs and trunk must take a great load in this throw, so there is considerable emphasis, even at general level, on resistance work for legs, trunk, shoulders/arms. The technical model will serve as a basis for the development of specific exercises by the coach. Figures 65 – 74 are examples of these.

fig.65

fig.66

fig.67

fig.68

fig.69

fig.70

fig.71

fig.72

fig.73

fig.74

THE JUMPS

It is tempting to see jumping as such a natural activity and so clearly leg-dependent, that development is frequently focussed on the strengthening of the legs, and on jumping itself. However, the truth is that technique in every jumping event is *not* altogether 'natural', and that while jumping efficiency *is* dependent upon the jumping leg, it is also dependent upon the 'posture' of the jumper, and on the use of other limbs.

Jumping might, then, be considered as a unique technical product of:-

TAKE-OFF:-   – Postural factors – alignment of trunk/hip, etc.
                                – Momentum factors – use of non-jumping legs and arms
                                – Jumping leg action – for height, for maintaining momentum, etc.

APPROACH:-   – Optimal velocity – for distance or height
                                – Running posture and transition to jump

FLIGHT:-   – Requirement of flight   – clear a bar
                                                    – remain balanced
                                                    – gain a landing advantage

It is my opinion that there is a basic posture model for take-off in all jumps (including the vault). The posture might best be thought of as similar to balancing a glass of water on the *crown* of one's head; back vertical and stiff (a strong back); the hips rolled under (i.e. *there is no arch in the back*); the free leg thigh is lifted up very fast by the hip – then is arrested abruptly when it is parallel with the ground.

The jumping model from the hip upwards is, therefore, almost identical in all jumps. It is absolutely essential that the trunk never bends or distorts over the hip, but that the 'glass of water' is balanced into and out of take-off. Some idea of this 'balance' may be achieved by performing a half squat action while the back is in contact with a wall (i.e. by sliding up the wall) (figure 75), or by stepping up onto a bench – without allowing the body weight to move forwards (i.e. lift directly upwards) (figure 76).

The basic model demands considerable static strength in the trunk – and a sound basis of general strength in the shoulders/back/hips/legs.

I would suggest that the athlete develops strength in the back and legs by orthodox means – with or without resistance, before moving to jumps practices per se.

Provided the athlete has such basic strength – and provided the coach is constantly observing that the athlete is maintaining the basic jumping posture, then activities such as the jumps decathlon (figure 77) may be used. In addition to these practices, there are, of course, games such as basketball, where the jumping action may be rehearsed many times in the course of play. Finally, there are traditional practices such as hopping, bounding, and running up hills or flights of steps.

 figure 75    figure 76

	1 Stand Long Jump	2 Stand Triple Jump	3 2 Hops Step & Jump	4 2 Hops 2 Steps & Jump	5 2 Hops 2 Steps 2 Jumps	6 5 Spring Jumps	7 Stand 4 Hops & Jump	8 Run 4 Hops & Jump	9 25 meter Hop	10 5 Stride Long Jump
100	3.73	10.51	13. 0	15.54	19.15	17.06	17.67	23.77	2.7	7.28
99	- -	10.43	12.90	15.46	18.99	16.91	17.52	23.62	-	- -
98	3.65	10.36	12.80	15.39	18.84	16.76	17.37	23.46	2.8	- -
97	- -	10.28	12.69	15.31	18.69	16.61	17.22	23.31	-	7.26
96	3.58	10.21	12.59	15.08	18.54	16.45	17.06	23.16	3.0	- -
95	- -	10.13	12.49	15.01	18.38	16.40	16.96	23.01	-	- -
94	3.50	10.05	12.39	14.88	18.23	16.25	16.86	22.85	3.1	7.23
93	- -	9.98	12.29	14.78	18.08	16.15	16.76	22.70	-	- -
92	3.42	9.90	12.19	14.68	17.93	16. 0	16.61	22.55	3.2	- -
91	- -	9.82	12.09	14.57	17.77	15.84	16.45	22.35	-	7.21
90	3.35	9.75	11.98	14.47	17.62	15.79	16.35	21.99	3.3	- -
89	- -	9.68	11.88	14.37	17.47	15.64	16.25	21.79	-	- -
88	3.27	9.60	11.78	14.27	17.32	15.54	16.15	21.64	3.4	7.18
87	- -	9.52	11.68	14.17	17.17	15.39	16. 0	21.48	-	- -
86	3.20	9.44	11.58	14.07	17.01	15.23	18.84	21.33	3.5	- -
85	- -	9.37	11.48	13.96	16.91	15.13	15.74	21.18	-	7.16
84	3.12	9.29	11.37	13.86	16.76	15.03	15.64	21.03	3.6	- -
83	- -	9.22	11.27	13.76	16.66	14.93	15.54	20.80	3.7	7.13
82	3.04	9.14	11.17	13.66	16.50	14.83	15.44	20.65	3.8	- -
81	- -	9.06	11.07	13.56	16.35	14.68	15.34	20.42	3.9	7.11
80	2.97	8.99	10.97	13.46	16.20	14.57	15.23	20.26	4.0	- -
79	- -	8.91	10.87	13.36	16.10	14.42	15.08	20.11	4.2	7.08
78	2.89	8.83	10.76	13.25	16.00	14.32	14.93	19.96	4.3	- -
77	- -	8.76	10.66	13.15	15.84	14.22	14.83	19.81	4.4	7.06
76	2.81	8.68	10.56	13.05	15.69	14.07	14.73	19.58	4.5	7.03
75	- -	8.61	10.46	12.95	15.54	13.96	14.63	19.43	4.6	7.01
74	2.74	8.53	10.36	12.85	15.39	13.86	14.47	19.20	4.7	6.95
73	2.69	8.45	10.26	12.75	15.23	13.71	14.32	19.04	4.8	6.90
72	2.66	8.38	10.15	12.64	15.13	13.61	14.22	18.89	4.9	6.85
71	2.64	8.30	10.05	12.53	15.03	13.51	14.12	18.74	5.0	6.80
70	2.61	8.22	9.95	12.42	14.88	13.41	14.02	18.59	5.1	6.75
69	2.59	8.15	9.85	12.31	14.73	13.25	13.86	18.44	5.2	6.70
68	2.56	8.07	9.75	12.19	14.63	13.10	13.71	18.28	5.4	6.62
67	2.53	8.00	9.65	12.09	14.47	13.00	13.61	18.13	5.5	6.55
66	2.51	7.92	9.55	11.98	14.32	12.90	13.51	17.98	5.6	6.47
65	2.48	7.84	9.44	11.88	14.22	12.80	13.41	17.75	5.7	6.40
64	2.46	7.77	9.34	11.78	14.07	12.69	13.30	17.60	5.8	6.32
63	2.43	7.69	9.24	11.68	13.96	12.59	13.20	17.37	5.9	6.24
62	2.41	7.61	9.14	11.58	13.81	12.49	13.10	17.22	6.0	6.17
61	2.38	7.54	9.04	11.48	13.71	12.34	12.95	17.06	6.1	6.09
60	2.36	7.46	8.94	11.37	13.56	12.19	12.80	16.91	6.2	6.01
59	2.33	7.39	8.83	11.27	13.41	12.03	12.64	16.76	6.3	5.94
58	2.31	7.31	8.73	11.17	13.25	11.88	12.49	16.53	6.5	5.86
57	2.28	7.23	8.63	11.07	13.10	11.78	12.39	16.38	6.6	5.79
56	2.26	7.16	8.53	10.97	12.95	11.68	12.29	16.15	6.7	5.71
55	2.23	7.08	8.45	10.87	12.80	11.58	12.19	16.00	6.8	5.63
54	2.20	7.01	8.38	10.76	12.64	11.48	12.09	15.84	6.9	5.56
53	2.18	6.93	8.30	10.66	12.49	11.37	11.98	15.69	7.0	5.48
52	2.15	6.85	8.22	10.56	12.34	11.27	11.58	15.54	7.1	5.41
51	2.13	6.78	8.15	10.46	12.19	11.17	11.42	15.39	7.2	5.33
50	2.10	6.70	8.07	10.36	12.03	11.07	11.27	15.23	7.3	5.25
49	2.08	6.62	8.00	10.26	11.88	10.97	11.17	15.08	7.4	5.18
48	2.05	6.55	7.92	10.15	11.73	10.87	11.07	14.93	-	5.13
47	2.03	6.47	7.84	10.05	11.58	10.76	10.97	14.78	7.5	5.07
46	2.00	6.40	7.77	9.95	11.42	10.66	10.82	14.63	-	5.02
45	1.98	6.32	7.69	9.85	11.27	10.56	10.66	14.47	7.7	4.97
44	1.95	6.24	7.61	9.75	11.17	10.46	10.51	14.32	-	4.92
43	1.93	6.17	7.54	9.65	11.07	10.36	10.36	14.17	7.8	4.87
42	1.90	6.09	7.46	9.55	10.97	10.26	10.21	14.02	-	4.82
41	1.87	6.01	7.39	9.44	10.87	10.15	10.05	13.86	7.9	4.77
40	1.85	5.94	7.31	9.34	10.76	10.05	9.90	13.71	-	4.72
39	1.82	5.86	7.23	9.24	10.66	9.95	9.75	13.56	8.0	4.67

	1 Stand Long Jump	2 Stand Triple Jump	3 2 Hops Step & Jump	4 2 Hops 2 Steps & Jump	5 2 Hops 2 Steps 2 Jumps	6 5 Spring Jumps	7 Stand 4 Hops & Jump	8 Run 4 Hops & Jump	9 25 meter Hop	10 5 Stride Long Jump
38	1.80	5.79	7.16	9.14	10.56	9.85	9.60	13.41	-	4.62
37	1.77	5.71	7.08	9.04	10.46	9.75	9.44	13.25	8.1	4.57
36	1.75	5.63	7.01	8.94	10.36	9.65	9.34	13.10	-	4.52
35	1.72	5.56	6.93	8.83	10.26	9.55	9.24	12.95	8.2	4.47
34	1.70	5.48	6.85	8.73	10.15	9.44	9.14	12.80	-	4.41
33	1.67	5.41	6.78	8.63	10.05	9.34	9.04	12.64	8.3	4.36
32	1.65	5.33	6.70	8.53	9.95	9.24	8.94	12.49	-	4.31
31	1.62	5.25	6.62	8.43	9.85	9.14	8.83	12.34	8.4	4.26
30	1.60	5.18	6.55	8.33	9.75	9.04	8.73	12.19	-	4.21
29	1.57	5.10	6.47	8.22	9.65	8.94	8.63	12.03	8.5	4.16
28	1.54	5.02	6.40	8.12	9.55	8.83	8.53	11.88	-	4.11
27	1.52	4.95	6.32	8.02	9.44	8.73	8.43	11.73	8.6	4.06
26	1.49	4.87	6.24	7.92	9.34	8.63	8.33	11.58	-	4.01
25	1.47	4.80	6.17	7.82	9.24	8.53	8.22	11.42	8.7	3.96
24	1.44	4.72	6.09	7.72	9.14	8.43	8.12	11.27	-	3.91
23	1.42	4.64	5.99	7.61	9.04	8.33	8.02	11.12	-	3.86
22	1.39	4.57	5.89	7.51	8.94	8.22	7.92	10.97	8.9	3.80
21	1.37	4.49	5.79	7.41	8.83	8.12	7.82	10.82	-	3.75
20	1.34	4.41	5.68	7.31	8.73	8.02	7.72	10.66	-	3.70
19	1.29	4.26	5.58	7.21	8.63	7.92	7.61	10.51	9.0	3.65
18	1.26	4.19	5.48	7.11	8.53	7.82	7.51	10.36	-	3.60
17	1.24	4.11	5.38	7.01	8.43	7.72	7.41	10.21	-	3.55
16	1.21	4.03	5.28	6.90	8.33	7.61	7.31	10.05	9.1	3.50
15	1.19	3.96	5.18	6.80	8.22	7.51	7.21	9.90	-	3.45
14	1.16	3.88	5.07	6.70	8.12	7.41	7.11	9.75	-	3.40
13	1.14	3.80	4.97	6.60	8.02	7.31	7.01	9.60	9.2	3.35
12	1.11	3.73	4.87	6.50	7.92	7.21	6.90	9.44	-	3.25
11	1.09	3.65	4.77	6.40	7.82	7.11	6.80	9.29	-	3.14
10	1.06	3.58	4.67	6.29	7.72	7.01	6.70	9.14	9.3	3.04
9	1.04	3.50	4.57	6.19	7.61	6.90	6.60	8.99	-	2.94
8	1.01	3.42	4.47	6.09	7.51	6.80	6.50	8.83	-	2.84
7	0.99	3.35	4.36	5.99	7.41	6.70	6.40	8.68	9.4	2.74
6	0.96	3.27	4.26	5.89	7.31	6.60	6.29	8.53	-	2.64
5	0.93	3.20	4.16	5.79	7.21	6.50	6.19	8.38	-	2.53
4	0.91	3.12	4.06	5.68	7.11	6.40	6.09	8.22	9.5	2.43
3	0.88	3.04	3.96	5.58	7.01	6.29	5.99	8.07	-	2.33
2	0.86	2.97	3.86	5.48	6.90	6.19	5.89	7.92	-	2.23
1	0.60	2.89	3.75	5.38	6.70	6.09	5.79	7.77	9.6	2.13

JUMPS DECATHLON SCORING TABLES

figure 77

HIGH JUMP

figure 78

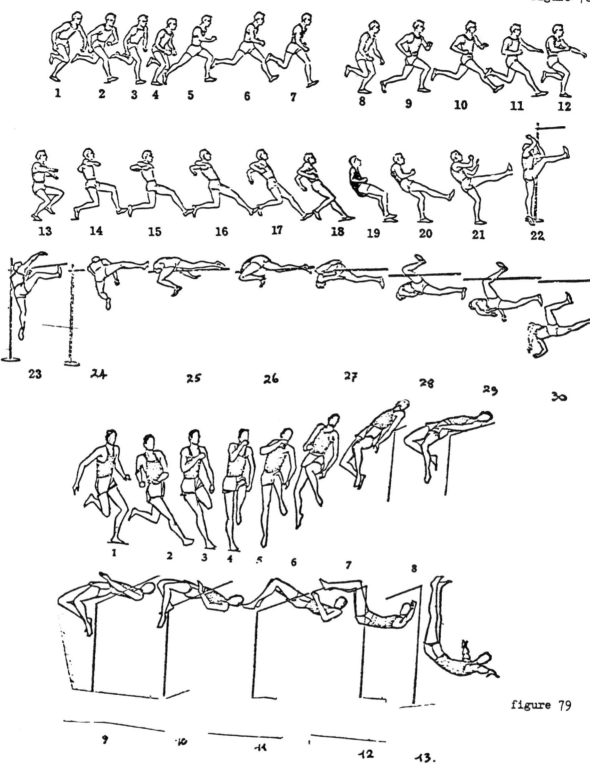

figure 79

The Basic Jump (standing)

It is of fundamental importance that the athlete's two objectives in this event are borne in mind – and that they are pursued in the order of priority shown here:-

1 Jump as high as possible

2 Avoid removing the bar.

Pursuit of the first objective involves consideration of *take-off* and *approach*, whilst pursuit of the second objective involves consideration of *flight*.

Take-off

I believe that the athlete should be aware at the outset that the free hip leads the total movement of take-off. Consequently, I suggest the following introductory practice:

(a) – Stand with hip/back/head as per basic Jumps posture.
   – The jumping foot is placed flat on the ground, ahead of the body, knee almost straight.
   – The weight is on the ball of the free foot – knee bent.
   – *Both hips are pressed forwards. (figure 80).*

figure 80

(b) The hips are pressed further forward with a short jabbing action of the right foot/knee.
   – The hips pull the free thigh/knee through fast.
   – The free knee straightens as it passes the jumping leg.

(c) The swinging action of the free leg *plus* a fast straightening action of the jumping leg lifts the athlete from the ground.

(d) The general feeling is one of jumping off the *heel* of the jumping foot.

(e) The head (glass of water!), back, hips and jumping leg should form a complete vertical line at take-off.

(f) The action may be made more elaborate by drawing back both elbows, thumbs turned in, and swinging the arms forwards and upwards with the free leg. The arm action should be fast and strong, with movement suddenly arrested when the arms reach shoulder height.

(g) The action may now be progressed to a 2 – 3 stride walk on heels (figure 81), then take-off (figure 82).

fig.81   fig.82   figure 83

This is, in effect, a straight-free-leg jumping technique, but it builds-in the hip movement – which is essential to all take-off techniques. The bent free leg action may easily be developed from this basic practice. (Heel behind knee!) (figure 83).

The Approach

The next stage of development is to build-up an approach. This is best done over 3 strides, then 5, 7 and so on.

I believe that no rotation should be introduced at this juncture. The athlete should practise jumping directly *upwards*, from this short approach. Practices such as jumping up to kick, knee, head or touch a hanging object (figure 84); or jumping upwards to clear a hurdle, or a series of hurdles (figure 85), should help develop the basic jumping model.

figure 84

figure 85

The main purpose of an approach is to 'compress the spring of the jumping leg'. This purpose is only served if the athlete can bring his weight *behind* the take-off foot prior to take-off, i.e. if the athlete can put himself into the starting position for the basic jump practice. The athlete attempts to do this by sitting back on his heels over the last 3 – 4 strides, keeping the back vertical (glass of water!); and pushing his hips forward with the take-off leg, as the foot is placed for take-off. The pulling back of the elbows may also help here.

The approach may also be performed in such a way that the athlete is inclined away from the bar in his take-off stride. This is achieved via a curved approach. Only the last 3 – 4 strides need be on a curve. This inclination means that as the athlete straightens to take-off, a favourable rotation is created, in flight. (figure 86)

figure 86

The speed of approach should be that which the athlete can use to his advantage. Straight approaches are normally 5 – 9 strides, curved approaches may be 7 – 14 strides.

The take-off point from a curve should be .50m – .75m from near upright along bar – and out from the bar. (figure 87)

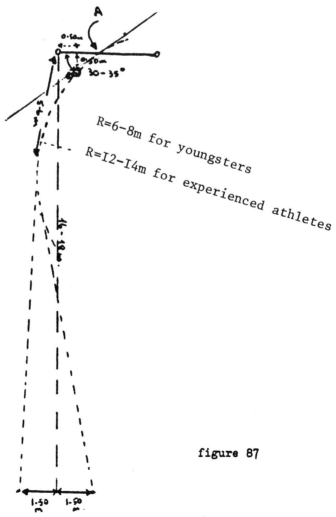

figure 87

24

The approach angle for a straight approach might be arrived at by the following method. (figures 88 and 89)

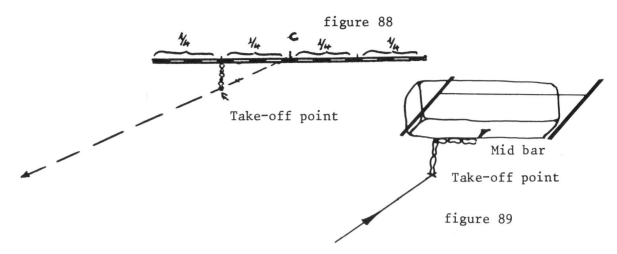

figure 88

Take-off point

Mid bar

Take-off point

figure 89

These take-off points are designed to pass the athlete over the bar at its lowest point (centre).

The curve is best arrived at by drawing or marking the curve on the floor/take-off pad. It is arbitrarily arrived at in most instances, but *consistency must be ensured*. The athlete *must* be sure of reaching his take-off point ready to jump. A check mark may be necessary at start of the curve.

Flight

Certain rotations and limb movements are sought in flight to ensure that the bar stays on, however, AT TAKE-OFF:-

— NO ROTATION MUST COME FROM THE JUMPING SIDE

— THE TRUNK MUST REMAIN VERTICAL

— THE SHOULDERS MUST REMAIN SQUARE (NATURAL POSITION) TO THE JUMPING LEG

— THE JUMPING FOOT MUST BE IN NATURAL ALIGNMENT WITH THE JUMPING LEG

This means that all rotation comes from either the non-jumping side.

figure 90

figure 91

— the straight free leg. (figure 90)

— the bent free leg brought across the body. (figure 91)

— the free side shoulder pulling *across* the body.

OR from the nature of the approach (curved).

I believe one of the best methods of introducing *straddle flight* (lay-out) is to perform a face vault over a bench/box/steeplechase barrier. Take-off leg remains bent (frog-like) throughout the clearance (knee up to arm pit). (figure 92) No attempt should be made to straighten the take-off leg once in the frog-like position. The athlete then attempts this over a slanted *elastic*. (figure 93) The elastic is gradually straightened – and a bar (hopefully round fibreglass) is introduced.

The Flop clearance might best be developed by jumping up onto a stacked landing area, to land on shoulders. *Then* practising the clearance action standing. (figure 94). The athlete now tries this off 3 – 5 – 7 strides, etc. (one foot). Over-emphasis of an *arch* is to be discouraged.

Note that the legs are recovered first by flexing at the hip – *then* by straightening the knee.

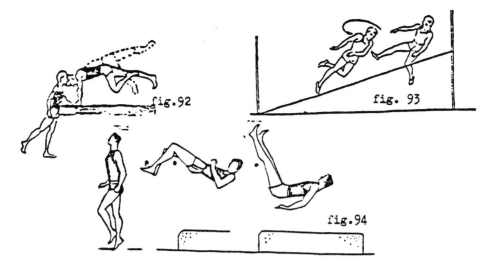

fig.92

fig. 93

fig.94

Conditioning

A sound basis of general strength is essential, plus work on sprints. Specific practices may be readily derived from consideration by the coach, of the basic technical model. Some examples are show in figures 95 – 107.

NOTE   A SAFE LANDING AREA AND CONSISTENT TAKE-OFF ARE PREREQUISITES TO OFFERING YOUNGSTERS THIS EVENT.

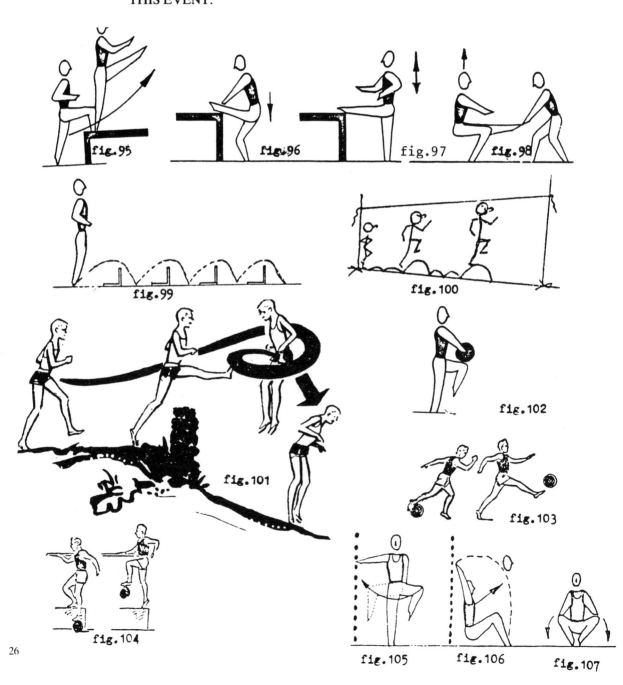

fig.95

fig.96

fig.97

fig.98

fig.99

fig.100

fig.101

fig.102

fig.103

fig.104

fig.105

fig.106

fig.107

LONG JUMP

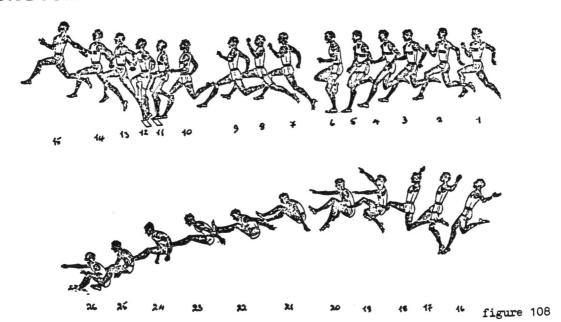

figure 108

The Basic Jump (standing)

The basic model posture should always be aimed for. Moreover, in flight, the athlete should attempt to maintain the head/trunk/hip alignment of the posture model (*i.e. no arching*). The action of the free thigh must be *very* fast, and emphasised as such throughout training – moreover, the *free knee must always be kept flexed until the athlete has taken-off* (heel behind knee).

The action of the arms is one of punching upwards with the arm on the take-off side – while 'lifting and balancing' with the other arm. The general sensation is one of lifting (adding momentum) with both arms.

The action of the jumping leg is one of *striking backwards and downwards*. The hip must not be allowed to collapse – nor must the trunk be 'distorted' – nor must the head tilt forwards, backwards, etc. The basic postural model *must* be kept.

The real problem for the athlete is not the component parts of this take-off, nor even the composite technique, but of performing these movements at high speed.

The coach may build up the technique in the standing or step-in form, but must quickly move to short approach work (5 – 11 strides). I suggest the following progression:-

(a) Standing with weight back on the ball of the free foot
Hips pressed forward
Take-off foot flat on the ground
Free knee bent

(b) Lift the free thigh fast + arm action
Jump into pit

i.e. This is a 'momentum' practice – but the take-off leg must work hard for lift.

The next stage is to step-in, allowing the athlete to add the 'strike' of the take-off leg (back and down!).

Now the practice moves to three strides – and the take-off should begin to look close to the technical model of the long jump. As more speed is added, the momentum and lifting aspects of the jump must be worked on *provided* that the athlete is also developing the backward striking action of the take-off leg.

Practices such as jumping over a hurdle, jumping to reach a suspended object and so on, might help here (figure 109).

← 3m →

figure 109

The Approach

The approach has two roles to fulfil:

1 To provide horizontal speed, which in turn, should provide horizontal distance. (The speed of take-off).

2 To 'compress the spring' of the jumping leg – which should provide vertical lift, thus adding height to the forward movement of take-off. (The angle of take-off).

An optimum speed is sought – and this over a distance of:-

Senior Men	22 – 24 strides
Senior Women	19 – 22 strides
Junior Men	20 – 24 strides
Intermed. Women	15 – 19 strides
Younger Men	17 – 20 strides
Younger Women	13 – 17 strides

The general feeling of the approach should be a combination of three phases:

1 Powerful acceleration

2 Preparation (awareness) for the final attack at the board

3 Attacking the board (postural adjustment for take-off).

All of this *must* be based on a consistency which is gradually added to as the athlete develops 'spatial judgement'.

Check marks may or may not be used by athletes.

I suggest the following method of developing the approach.

(a)   Aiming to jump from a point beyond the board (i.e. *not* jumping from the board) – an approximate distance of approach is estimated according to the number of strides to be used – say 1 stride = roughly 2 metres.

(b)   The athlete counts '1 – 2 – 3' etc. every time the take-off foot strikes the ground (i.e. he would take off on '10' for a 19 stride approach). He then runs and jumps on '10'. The coach notes the take-off point. (figure 110)

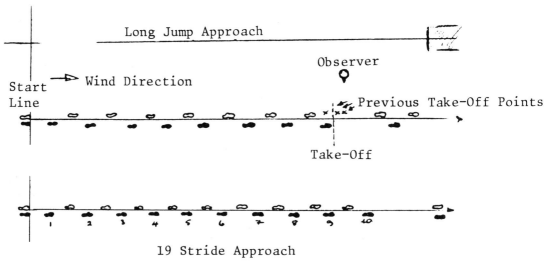

figure 110

(c)   This is repeated 4 – 6 times, as the coach notes the general area of take-off.

(d)   The approach is then measured from start to the farthest limit of this area closest to the pit.

(e)   This distance is now measured back from the board, and is used as the initial run-up (approach) on subsequent occasions. It will be slightly altered on each occasion according to wind, weather and track surface.

The rhythm of the approach might be as follows. (figure 111)

ACCELERATE	PREPARE	ATTACK
1 and 2 and 3 and 4 and 5	and 1 and 2 and	1 and 2 and 3

The athlete will learn to make stride length adjustments to 'home in' on the board (spatial judgement), simply with continued experience of jumping. However, low hurdling and the stride adjustments this requires – or running to strike a line or mark with either foot, may well help the learning process.

I believe that the attack over the last strides to take-off should be made with the hips/back/head in alignment, very close to that of the basic jumping posture, and that the attack should be with a powerful, high but fast knee lift.

28

Flight

The athlete must attempt to maintain balance in flight, so that he can effect a good leg shoot prior to landing. This being the case, I suggest that the athlete attempts to maintain the hips/back/head alignment of take-off – and *does not arch the back*.

Flight technique might best be developed by performing a 'stride jump' (figure 112). The athlete holds the free leg in its take-off position – then draws up the take-off leg, extending both legs prior to landing.

figure 112

The next development might be to 'run' in the air – prior to leg shoot (figure 113). I think that it is best here for the athlete to think of stamping down and back with the free foot heel, as the take-off leg is brought through bent. The take-off leg is then extended for landing and the free leg is brought through bent, then extended to join the take-off leg.

By this time, the thighs and trunk are brought together – *heels high*.

The leg shoot (high heels) idea might be more easily learned if the athlete has to clear a sand 'wall' (figure 114).

figure 113

figure 114

Recovery

The athlete achieves this either by pivoting over the feet (collapsing knees and throwing chest to knees) (figure 115) or by 'sliding through' with the hips (figure 116). Some athletes have attempted to quickly collapse *one* leg and slide round to that side.

I have found that one of the best ways of practising this phase is to jump *down* sand dunes.

figure 115

figure 116

Conditioning

Clearly, this athlete must have a very good background of running training (that of a 200m athlete) – plus a high general strength of shoulders/trunk/hips/legs. Specific practices similar to those shown in figures 117 – 159 are based on the technical model of take-off, and the demands of flight. The coach will develop a large selection of these.

fig.117   fig.118   fig.119   fig.120   fig.146   fig.147   fig.148   fig.149

fig.121   fig.122   fig.123   fig.150   fig.151

fig.124   fig.125   fig.126   fig.152   fig.153

fig.128   fig.130   fig.127   fig.129   fig.131   fig.154   fig.155

fig.132   fig.133   fig.134   fig.135   fig.136   fig.156

fig.137   fig.138   fig.139   fig.140   fig.141

fig.142   fig.143   fig.144   fig.145   fig.157   fig.158   fig.159

TRIPLE JUMP

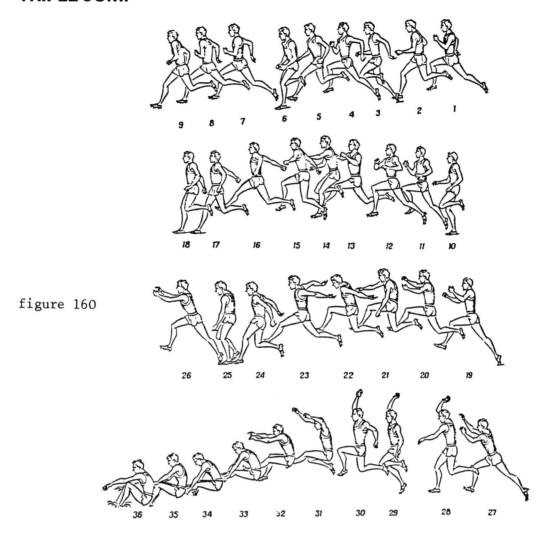

figure 160

The Basic Jump (standing)

The old title for this event was the 'Hop – Step and Jump', a title which, although describing the basic actions of the three phases, is less appropriate than the picture created by 'Triple Jump'.

The basic jumping posture for head/trunk/hip still holds good – and throughout each phase of take-off, flight, and re-take-off, this posture should be maintained. Another feature worth building-in at the outset is that of 'flat foot landings'. Thus, we have the coaching point of 'flat back, flat feet'.

I have found it useful to develop the technical model as follows, because I believe that the rhythm and 'feel' of the event should precede the building-up of the 'striking' action of the legs.

(a) The athlete stands with his dominant foot on a lane line at the edge of the track.

(b) He hops onto the next line and balances there.

(c) He jumps to land on the other foot on the next lane line.

(d) He jumps again to land with both feet on the next line.

(e) Having repeated this several times, he is asked to jump as high as possible from each line (except the last) – with a vigorous free hip/thigh lift, and swing of both arms.

(f) He is now taken to a special grid (figure 161) and triple jumps from line to line, with a 3 – 5 stride approach.

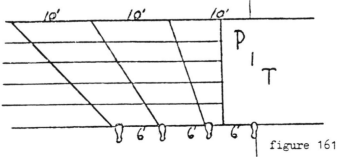

figure 161

31

(g)   His progression along the grid is noted, and the distances marked from a take-off board (or painted line) with shoes, etc.

(h)   The athlete now off 5 – 7 strides, triple jumps from shoe to shoe – landing in the pit.

(i)   By this time the 'striking' or 'clawing' action of the jumping leg at each take-off should be emphasised, but it is quite possible that the athlete will develop this himself. (figure 162)

figure 162

(j)   The athlete now begins to increase his approach run distance. (see Long Jump for development of approach run)

Once the athlete reaches the stage of full approach jumps, it is essential that he is also involved in an organized programme of conditioning for legs and back.

I like the concept advanced by a Hungarian Triple Jump coach, that the 'hop' phase be thought of as the last part of the approach, because very often the athlete, in attempting to make the hop a powerful jump, collapses on landing.

The phases of the jump are seldom equal, in fact. Generally speaking, the ratio is 35% – 30% – 35%, with the average of the three phases being roughly 70% of the athlete's best long jump. For example, if the athlete's best long jump was 6.00m, then the average of the three phases would be 70% of 6.00m = 4.20m. In other words, the ideal jump would be 3 x 4.20m = 12.60m. The hop phase should be 35% of this = 4.41m; the step should be 30% =3.75m; and the jump, again at 35% = 4.41m. The coach would mark these points with shoes, etc.

Essential to a sound take-off and flight, is a balanced, flat-backed posture.

Essential to the maintenance of forward momentum are active leg strike, and an optimum speed of approach.

Essential to covering ground with each phase, are the lifting action of the swinging arms, the basic jumping posture, and the backward and downward strike of the take-off leg(s).

Flight and landing considerations are very similar to those of Long Jump, but because landing is normally 'flatter', the recovery is more likely to be a 'sliding' type.

Conditioning

This is a very tough event physically, and the athlete must, in addition to a sound background of running (200m type training), be very strong in the back, hips and legs. It is not sufficient to rely on general-type training, and the athlete *must* be encouraged to do specific practices based on the technical model and energy demands of the event. The coach will readily devise these, but figures 163 – 177 may serve as a guide.

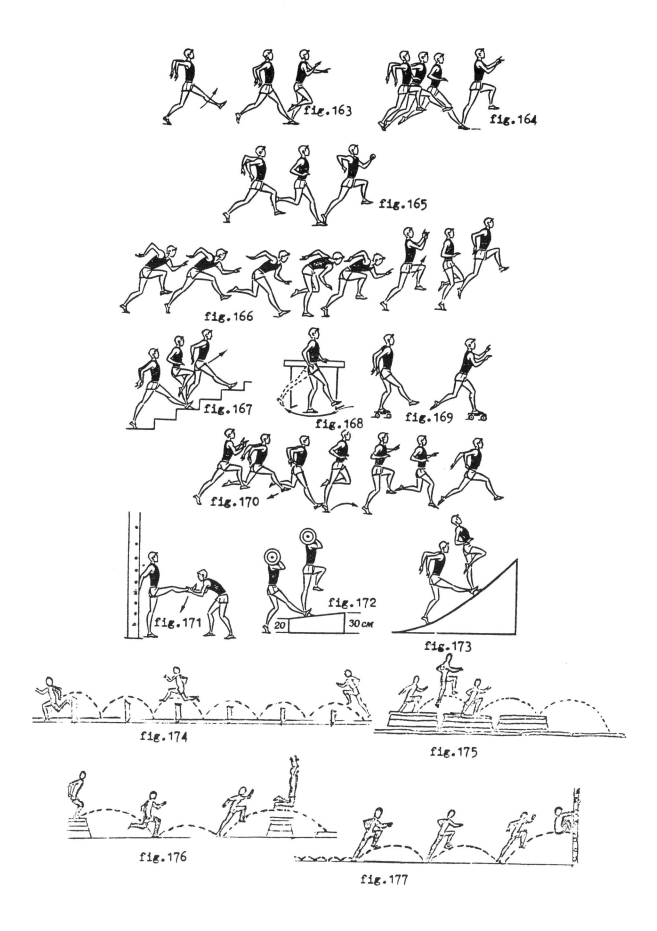

fig.163

fig.164

fig.165

fig.166

fig.167

fig.168

fig.169

fig.170

fig.171

fig.172

20   30 см

fig.173

fig.174

fig.175

fig.176

fig.177

POLE VAULT

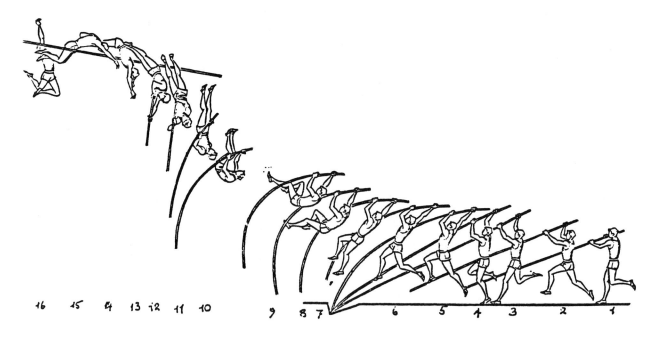

figure 178

The Basic Vault (can only be done if preceded by a short approach)

The event, at a relatively early stage of competition, requires the use of a flexible (fibreglass) pole.

However I shall assume here that the athlete will start vaulting with a rigid pole.

The landing area for vaulting *must be safe to land on in relation to the height vaulted.*

Introduce the event as near the ground as possible in case the student fails to take his bodyweight.

The introduction of the athlete to vaulting might take the following course for a right handed vaulter:

(a) Grip with *right* hand at between forehead height and arms length height from the bottom of the pole – left hand 30 centimetres lower. Carry pole on *right* side of the body.

(b) With a short run, place the pole as near vertically as possible and swing on the *right* side of the pole, landing lightly on the feet.

(c) Practise repeatedly, building confidence and aiming for greater distance and neat gymnastic control.

The action is rather like paddling an Indian canoe.

Suitable facilities for this exercise are two linked 8" x 8' x 4' (20cms x 2.50 x 1.50) crash mats (foam rubber filled) or a well dug large long jump pit.

(d) An elastic bar may be introduced, starting at 20cm. and raising to *no more than 1 metre*. With distance in mind the following may be introduced to develop the picture of the vault as one of:-

    i   swinging to the pole
    ii tucking the knees up to the chest
    iii crossing the free leg over the jumping leg
    iv passing over the bar face down (figure 182)

Other valuable activities to maintain interest, develop technique and strength or to help the athlete co-ordinate the movement are:-

Fig. 179   swinging from cushion to cushion

Fig. 180   the Burkitt Method, i.e. the coach grips the pole, already planted, and swings the athlete through.

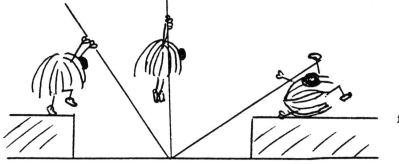

figure 179

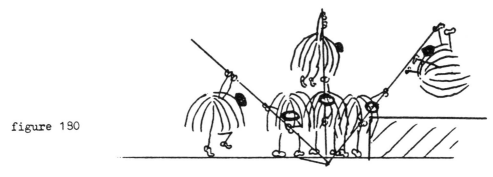

figure 180

Before progressing to a competition landing area the athlete must first have some idea of the carry and plant. The right hand holds the pole in undergrasp, the left in overgrasp, and the pole is carried as in figure 181.

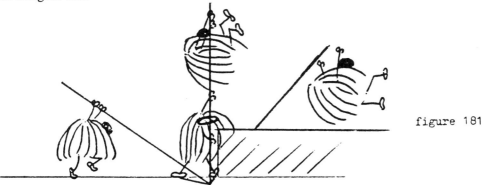

figure 181

The planting action begins as the left foot hits the ground for the last stride but one. The pole is pushed forward with the left arm to full extension and the right hand brought to forehead height. On the final stride the right hand is pressed as high as possible.

figure 182

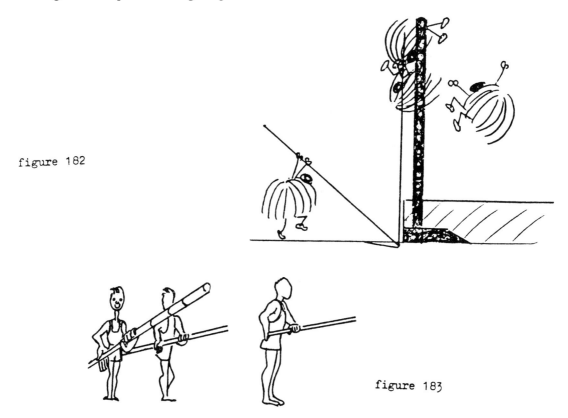

figure 183

The movement, whilst not difficult, is a problem of timing to begin with, and the athlete will need considerable practice.

I suggest that the planting practices be done into sand rather than a box, to familiarise the athlete with the action *and* the shock of the pull on the shoulders at take-off. Right hand, head and left foot should be vertically aligned (figure 184).

The athlete may now return to a version of the Burkitt exercise where he carries and plants the pole, and the coach pulls the pole through. Very quickly, the coach assumes the role of the pole-catcher, and the athlete builds confidence to complete the whole vault on his own.

Right hand action is like a right uppercut starting and finishing
here   here

Push pole forward

Now lift it up

Think about a long jump take-off

figure 184

figure 185

The athlete can now practise on the full landing area, lifting hips above shoulders.

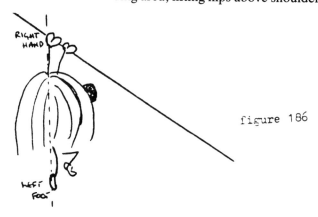

RIGHT HAND

LEFT FOOT

figure 186

and passing the bar face down.

(e)   These movements may be elaborated on further by emphasising:-
a take-off similar to that of long jump (up and out)
a posture at take-off consistent with the basic jumps posture
a pull-push action between ii and iii.

Note. When vaulting on a full landing area, it is better and safer if the vaulter lands on his back. At no time encourage the vaulter to land on his seat or base of his spine.

The athlete will very quickly clear around 2.50 – 3.00m with this practice.
The athlete should now be establishing an approach run (15 – 21 strides), along similar lines to the method used for long jump. He should plant the pole in the sand to allow for errors of spatial judgement in the learning stages.

As the athlete progresses towards 3.00m on the rigid pole, he should be encouraged towards the flexible pole. Development here might take the following course:-
(a)   From 3 strides the athlete plants the pole into a towel, taking off (gently) as in the long jump but with the right arm locked above the head. The whole body movement (transmitting power through the right hand) drives the towel forward.

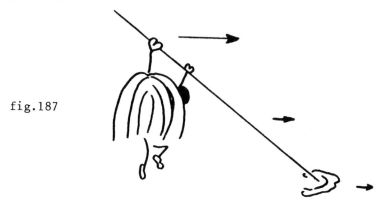

fig.187

(b) Replace the towel with a half car inner tube lightly filled with sand and tied at each end.
A note of caution:- If the resistance is too great and it does not move easily, the athlete's feet can swing from under him and he will fall on his back. Although in the complete vault it is this very action that will help him get upside down!
The weighted inner tube or wooden "box" must continue to be driven forward, the right arm and trunk action as one in a locked position.

(c) Increase the weight of the inner tube gradually.

(d) Increase the length of the run-up – measure and transfer to the pole vault run-up proper.

(e) With vaulting for distance in mind, vault into the landing area proper using a low grip and a 4 meter fibreglass pole 20lbs. below bodyweight. (One cannot be dogmatic here. Children will require a shorter pole and good sense is required by the coach).
After take-off, press the pole forward (or the body back) with the right arm pressing down the length of the pole, compressing the pole. This action causes a reaction – the knees come up! The left arm acts to control the movement. Do not push with the left arm. To repeat, it is like paddling an "Indian canoe".

(f) "Inch" the grip higher and gradually the pole will bend as a result of bodyweight and the pressure applied by the right hand.

When a 50° bend has been achieved, move to a pole of the same length but 15lbs. below bodyweight and use the same handgrip. "Inch" the grip up until 50° bend has been reached. (The handgrip will be approximately 5cms. above the previous pole.)

Because a pole is more difficult to bend when held at lower than the advised grip, it is not always necessary to vault on a pole marked to the vaulter's bodyweight.

A vaulter of 150lbs. who is a slow runner may vault on a 140 lb. pole as long as his top hand is 10cms. or more below the advised grip.

Longer poles built by some companies are more resistant, i.e. a 4.00 metre 140lb. pole is equal to a 4.30 metre 130lb. pole of the same make.

BOTH THESE STATEMENTS ARE A POLE VAULTER'S ROUGH GUIDE.

The event is an individual affair and must be treated as such.

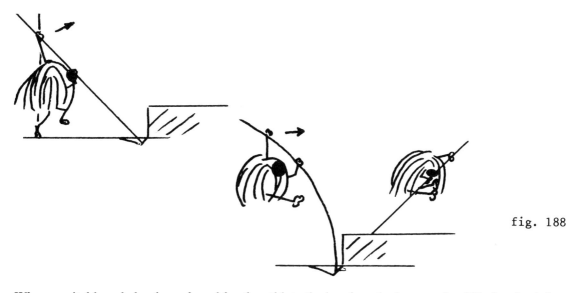

fig. 188

When a suitable pole has been found for the athlete the bend can be increased to 90°. An elastic bar may be introduced at this point. The athlete must:-
  i   Lift the pole high as he plants fast
  ii   Take off as per long jump, driving up and out
  iii Transmit his power and momentum through the right arm, controlling his balance with the left
  iv   *Then* rock back – shoulders down, thighs/hips up
  v   Keep lifting the hips until he is *along* the pole – so that when it straightens, he is thrown upwards,not outwards
  vi   Turn very late – (after the pole has begun to straighten)
  vii Pull-push off the top of the pole
  viii Curl round the bar and lift the elbows clear

This event requires great courage on the flexible pole and the coach must bear this in mind. These poles *can* break – and this is a traumatic experience for an athlete. A vaulter feels as if he is being lifted, but with a sensation of falling backwards as the pole bends with his rock back. Patience and understanding are great attributes for the coach working with a vaulter. (PERRIN simulator)

Conditioning

The vaulter is an athlete and gymnast. In fact, he is normally a good all-round athlete (Superstar!). He must have a background of running and a great deal of strength relative to his body weight. General strength work is not sufficient. Enormously strong pectorals and grip are required and the athlete must work on specific practices based on the technical model of the event. Some examples are given here to offer some guidance to the coach, (figure 190 – 204). Olympic gymnastic work on rings and parallel bars, coupled with weight training – especially for the upper body.

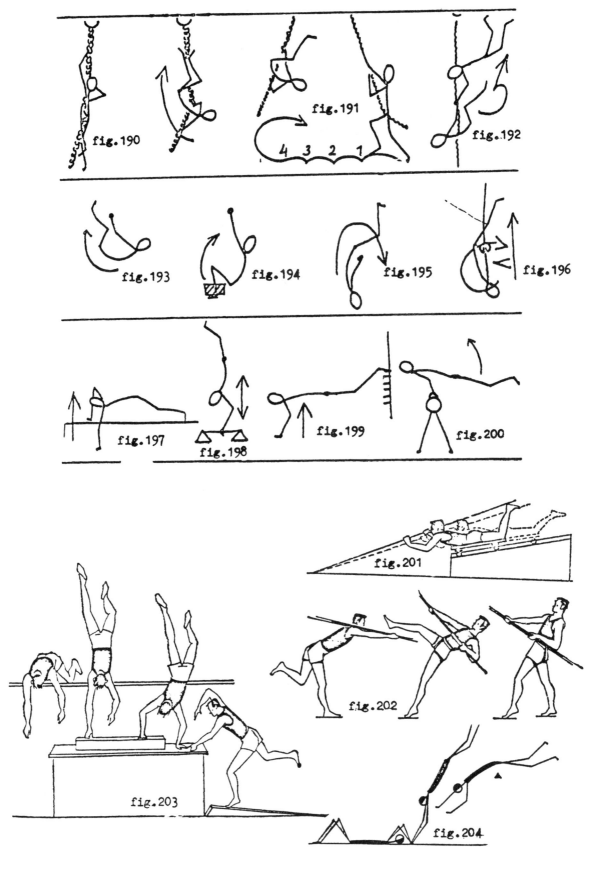

fig.190
fig.191
fig.192
fig.193
fig.194
fig.195
fig.196
fig.197
fig.198
fig.199
fig.200
fig.201
fig.202
fig.203
fig.204

TRACK EVENTS

I believe that the running events should be considered as technical events. It is true, of course, that running is a 'natural activity', but *efficient* running requires technical instruction.

Observation of a group of youngsters running, will clearly demonstrate the variety of movements which come under the heading of 'running'. The variety is due to a complex of reasons, such as poor motor co-ordination; and poor mobility or strength, and the resultant compensatory actions.

I believe that the technical development of an athlete's running action should advance *in* three stages.

1 Development of general fitness – strength, mobility, endurance.

2 Development of a sound and efficient running technique, together with specialised elements such as hurdling, water jump clearance – and starting.

3 The progressive development of speed, and specific endurance, with parallel development of relaxation, rhythm and economy of effort.

In addition, it should be remembered that these stages are annually re-cycled, with the coach constantly aware of the need to restructure the technical aspects of running, as the athlete's fitness shifts its emphasis in specific strength, etc. against speed and on all-round sophistication born of competition experience.

General fitness development is covered elsewhere. However, the second and third stages of technical development will be considered under the headings:

Sprints
Hurdles
Distance (and Steeplechase)
Relays

These events will be followed by the walks and the combined events.

SPRINTING

figure 205a

Sprinting has been described as a multi-strike event. This is quite an apt description for 'setting the scene' of the technique, because the leg action is one of striking or clawing the ground. However, to concentrate on this item solely is to forget that the total technique of sprinting encompasses –

  i   Posture
  ii Arm action
  iii Leg action.

The total technique is, of course, based on sound general strength of arm/shoulder, trunk, and leg/hip.

Posture (see figure 205a)

The athlete should always concentrate on *running* tall – *with eyes looking directly forward, chin down – never up*! The trunk, then, is fairly erect, with the *crown* of the head reached upwards, *not* the forhead.

The shoulders should remain square to the direction of the run. In other words, there should be no shoulder rolling, or twisting of the trunk.

The hips should feel raised or 'lifted' – and *never* low, because this will lead to a 'sitting' action in running.

This 'strong' posture gives a sound 'chassis' for the 'motor' of arms and legs to work on.

Coaching advice may be "run tall" and "run with a glass of water on your head", "run light and lifted", "run your hips high", "run as if pulled by an invisible cord straight down the track", "straight back, chin down".

It is very important that there is no distortion of trunk/hips, as this will lead to absorption of energy rather than its transference to the track for propulsion.

Arm Action (see figure 205a)

"Fast arms lead fast legs"

"Fast arms mean short levers and relaxation".

These two coaching adages carry a lot of truth, and the coach would do well to bear them in mind.

Maintaining the arm action as a short lever movement might be thought of as an attempt to move *the upper arm* through its wide range, with the elbow always flexed.

The elbow angle may be arrived at by the athlete resting his thumb on his hip. The athlete should always think of maintaining this angle as the arm swings backwards and forwards. The angle must *never* open wider

wider than this (i.e. approx. 90°). If it closes, it does so in the forward movement, and then almost as an effect of momentum. (see figure 205a) The athlete should feel that the hand comes no further back than the hip: and that it comes no higher in front than the shoulder.

The athlete should also feel that the elbows brush his vest in moving forwards and backwards – and that they are *not* sticking out to the side like wings!

The arm action must be well-drilled, with the movement 'coming from the shoulder'.

Tension or fatigue work *against* speed by reducing the athlete's capacity to relax. The situation may be improved by ensuring adequate strength and specific endurance in the shoulders and arms. Relaxation is, however, a fairly abstract concept when there is pressure on in a race, even when the athlete has adequate strength and endurance. Hence the use of such equipment as speed ball, elastic resistance and so on, to oblige the athlete to relax in a situation requiring rhythm and co-ordination at speed.

Leg Action (see figure 205a)

The leg action might best be described as a 'striking and pushing' the ground from under to behind the athlete.

The 'striking' action is very active and commences the moment the thigh is driven downwards and backwards from its high recovery position, parallel to the track. In other words, the foot is not laid on the track, it is almost 'thrown' at the running surface.

The 'pushing' action is felt by the athlete to be as if his foot has stuck to the ground behind his body. The thigh's action in the 'strike' continues as the hip completes its extension. The next joint to extend is the knee – and finally the ankle, as the foot 'flicks away' the track.

Another sensation with which the athlete will become familiar is one of bouncing *from* the ball of one foot *onto* the ball of the other. In fact, acceleration will be felt as a greater sensation of pressure on the balls of the feet.

The recovery action should be thought of as 'high and fast'.

Starting

figure 205b

The start is *not* a separate part of the sprint race. From start to finish is *one* whole – and the athlete should simply see the start as a means of 'getting into his running' as fast as possible. (figure 205b)

The start position must be comfortable, both in the 'On your marks' and 'Set' positions. It must also allow the athlete to *move his arms first and fast into the sprint arm action,* and to produce a powerful 'strike-push' leg action to drive him down the track. Key thoughts are –

   i   Fast arms
   ii Eyes down – chest low
   iii Strike – push
   iv *Run – don't explode.*

Foot placement may be arrived at by the following rule of thumb (figure 206).

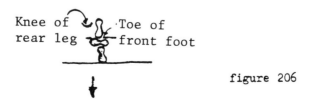

figure 206

This should provide high hips with weight forward over the front foot in the set position; front knee approx. 90°; rear knee approx. 120°. 'Blockless' starts may encourage the feeling of *running* from the start.

Blocks normally have a shallow angle at the front block (30° – 45° to track) and a steep angle at the rear block (60° – 80° to track).

The weight should be borne equally by the arms. To lean too heavily to one side will cause the athlete to push out in that direction at the start.

Bend Running

The athlete should hold the inside of his lane, leaning into the bend. The right arm slightly crosses the chest, the left arm is slightly dropped.

Bend Starting

The athlete should align his blocks/start to make the longest possible tangent with a point roughly 25cm into his lane from the inside of the track (figure 207).

figure 207

Finishing

ALWAYS RUN THROUGH THE FINISHING LINE. AVOID DIPPING OR DIVING AT THE FINISH.

Conditioning

On the basis of general strength, endurance and mobility, the athlete, working to the technical model of sprinting, may work through various specific practices. The striking action may be developed by hops and bounding (figure 208).

figure 208

The pushing action may be developed by harness-type runs. The speed of leg recovery, and the bouncing action, may be developed by 'innervation' practices such as the 'skip drills' (figure 209).

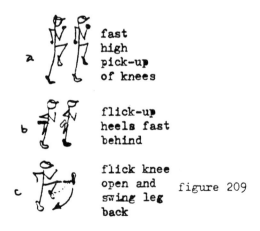

a   fast high pick-up of knees

b   flick-up heels fast behind

c   flick knee open and swing leg back   figure 209

Some other sprints conditioning exercises are illustrated in figures 210 – 223.

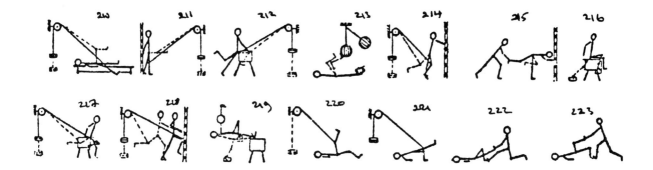

Technique runs are used to isolate specific points of sprinting technique. These *must* allow the athlete to progress the speed of execution – hence increasing speed over the final 25% – 30% of the training distance.

Acceleration development may be done from blocks or from standing – over 20 – 60 metres. A modification of this is 'in – out – in' (e.g. sprint 30m; decelerate 30m; sprint 30m).

Speed development – rolling start runs, where athlete must *hold maximum speed* for 20 – 40 metres.

Speed endurance development – running 'over distance' e.g. 60 secs. runs; 250m, 300m, 500m; repeated 10 – 12 times with intervals permitting no loss of speed in successive runs, at a speed of 60% – 80% max.

– running 60% – 80% racing distance in 2 – 4 sets of 5 – 2 repetitions at 80% – 95% max., with 2 – 3 mins recovery between repetitions, and 5 – 15 mins. between sets.

Strength endurance development – running in 'resisted' situations, e.g. harness runs, hill sprints, 'skip drills' over 200m etc.

Competition development – handicap runs, time trials over 60m – 250m (100m/200m athletes), 250m – 500m (400m); 'section runs' (e.g. first 120m of 200m; middle 250m of 400m; etc; COMPETITIONS THEMSELVES.

HURDLES

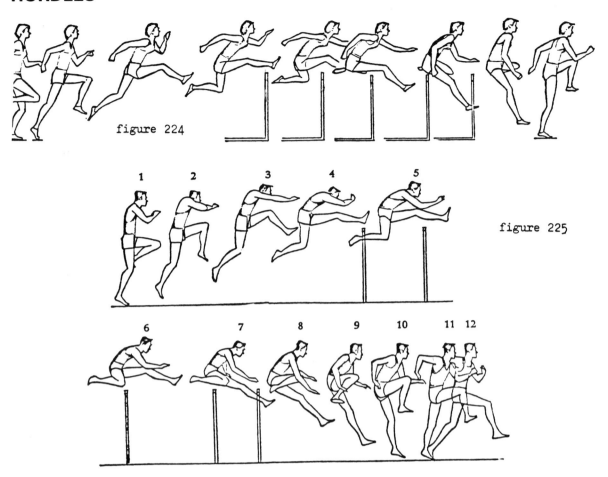

figure 224

figure 225

Hurdling is, because of its technical and energy demands, an exciting and challenging group of events in its own right, and an excellent adjunct to the athlete's training for other disciplines. The technical component of hurdling is clearly much greater than in sprinting, yet *the concept of the hurdles race must be one of a sprint,* with adjustment for each hurdle. Unlike the field events' techniques, the technical model is repeated several times in the event. This creates a unique set of technical problems, because although the demand for technical precision is constant throughout a race, the situation-complex of speed, rhythm and endurance is changing – and consequently technical training must include work to develop –

— maintenance of balance in the latter stages of a high-hurdles race, where the hurdles 'appear to be closer together' – i.e. the athlete must learn to move the limbs faster.

— maintenance of rhythm as fatigue sets in with the low/intermediate hurdles, i.e. the athlete must learn a smooth transition to an increased number of strides between hurdles.

— maintenance of rhythm and balance in adverse conditions, i.e. the athlete must develop spatial judgement to regulate his stride length.

Such work must be accompanied by a progressive conditioning programme on the one hand, and development of the athlete's flat-racing speed and speed endurance on the other. I see the total scheme of things as follows:-

HURDLING DEVELOPMENT	RUNNING DEVELOPMENT	CONDITIONING DEVELOPMENT
1	Technique running and general endurance	General mobility and general basic strength
2 Establish concept of event		
3 Develop technical model	Technique running and specific endurance	Specific mobility; elastic strength
	Sprinting speed	Specific mobility; specific strength
4 Develop special running	Speed, speed endurance	
5 Competitions	Competitions 100m – 400m	Recreation

The 'sprints' section deals with the 'running development' aspect, with the exception of 'specific endurance' – which is discussed here. The conditioning development aspect is covered in the section on 'CONDITIONING' – with the exception of 'specific mobility', which with some specific strength practices, is also discussed here. This leaves 'hurdling development', which I'd like to consider in some detail.

Establishing the Concept

The sprint (high) hurdles have a rhythm of three strides between hurdles. It is possible from the very outset to have athletes sprinting over 30 – 40m with a cane or flattened barrier coinciding with this pattern (figure 226). Very quickly, the barrier can be raised to knee height with the athlete always endeavouring to concentrate on sprinting rather than going over barriers. At the same time, the barriers can be gradually increased in their distance apart. Some authorities recommend that 4 strides be used between barriers in the learning stages, for maintenance of sprinting rhythm and for learning to hurdle from either leg.

A series of lanes can be used through which the athlete may progress (figure 227).

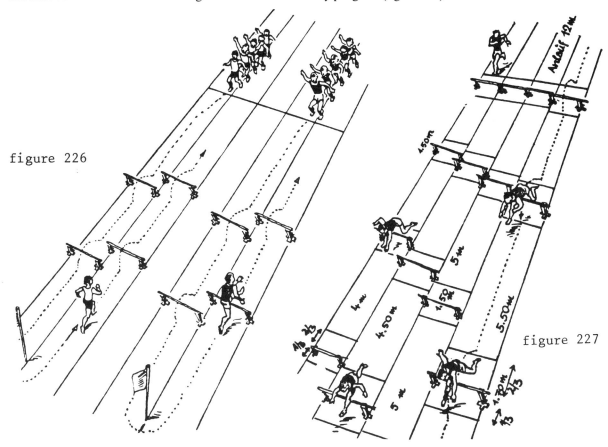

figure 226

figure 227

Once the first lane has been cleared – with athletes progressing to lanes 2, 3, etc., then the first lane can be used as a further progression, i.e.

The athlete should be emphasising –

(a) Fast controlled sprinting – picking the knees up *fast*.

(b) *Pushing over* the space where the barrier lies. This may be helped by hurdling across imaginary 'ditches' symbolised by chalked lines (figure 228).

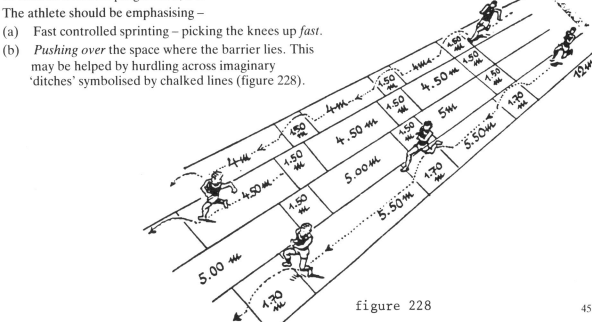

figure 228

45

I must stress here that the principle to be followed is 'adjust the event to the athlete – *then* adjust the athlete to the event'.

The concept must never be lost to the athlete, even when he is concentrating on the 'technical model'. The coach must constantly refer the athlete to the concept. Thus, as the barrier is raised above knee height, it becomes essential to concentrate on the 'leading leg' part of the technical mode. The coach, in developing this part via practices and drills must bring the athlete back to the 'concept' by having the athlete run over the hurdles as before – but incorporating the newly developed lead leg. As the barrier increases in height and is spaced further, the next part of the technical model requiring consideration is the 'trail leg'; on increasing height and spacing again – the upper body action ('dipping') is focussed upon; and finally, come the arms. *Throughout,* the 'concept' is stressed – and gradually the barrier heights and spacings assume the 'official' figures (figure 229).

Of assistance in establishing the concept is listening to the rhythm of the feet on the track. The athlete is seeking to keep the rhythm as close as possible to the regular sprinting, with very little interruption for barrier clearance. The event must *never* become a series of high jumps!

Again, a valuable guide to the coach is to watch the athlete's height throughout the run. There should be very little elevation at each barrier – and the coach should have the impression of the line of progression of the athlete's head being parallel with the ground (figures 224, 225).

The relatively flat and fast passage of the athlete over the hurdle is the ratio of his take-off – hurdle distance, compared with his hurdle-landing distance. A sound rule of thumb in that the ratio should be 2:1 (figure 227).

	Age	Distance	Height	Start to First Hurdle	Between Hurdles	Last Hurdle to Finish	Number of Hurdles	Standard Track Marking	Toppling Weight
BOYS	17, 18 & 19	110m	0.99m	13.72m	9.14m	14.02m	10	Blue	3.6kg
	17, 18 & 19	200m	0.762m	18.29m	18.29m	17.10m	10	Purple	3.6kg
	17, 18 & 19	400m	0.914m	45m	35m	40m	10	Green	3.6kg
	17, 18 & 19	60m Indoor	0.99m	13.72m	9.14m	9.72m	5	—	3.6kg
	15, 16	100m	0.914m	13m	8.5m	10.5m	10	Yellow	2.7kg
	15, 16	400m	0.84m	45m	35m	40m	10	Green	2.7kg
	15, 16	60m Indoor	0.914m	13m	8.5m	13m	5	—	2.7kg
	13, 14	80m	0.84m	12m	8m	12m	8	Black	2.7kg
	11, 12	80m	0.762m	12m	8m	12m	8	Black	2.7kg
•	11, 12	75m	0.682m	11.5m	7.5m	11m	8	Orange	2.7kg
•	11, 12	70m	0.682m	11m	7m	10m	8	Pink	2.7kg
•	10 and under	60m	0.682m	10.5m	6.5m	10.5m	7	None	2.7kg
•	10 and under	60m	0.61m	10m	6m	14m	7	None	2.7kg
GIRLS	17, 18 & 19	100m	0.84m	13m	8.5m	10.5m	10	Yellow	3.6kg
	17, 18 & 19	400m	0.762m	45m	35m	40m	10	Green	3.6kg
	17, 18 & 19	60m Indoor	0.84m	13m	8.5m	13m	5	—	3.6kg
	15, 16	80m	0.762m	12m	8m	12m	8	Black	2.7kg
	15, 16	100m	0.762m	13m	8.5m	10.5m	10	Yellow	2.7kg
	15, 16	200m	0.762m	16m	19m	13m	10	White	2.7kg
	15, 16	300m	0.762m	50m	35m	40m	7	Green	2.7kg
	15, 16	400m	0.762m	45m	35m	40m	10	Green	2.7kg
	15, 16	60m Indoor	0.762m	12m	8m	16m	5	—	2.7kg
	15, 16	60m Indoor	0.762m	13m	8.5m	13m	5	—	2.7kg
	13, 14	75m	0.762m	11.5m	7.5m	11m	8	Orange	2.7kg
	13, 14	60m Indoor	0.762m	11.5m	7.5m	18.5m	5	—	2.7kg
	11, 12	70m	0.682m	11m	7m	10m	8	Pink	2.7kg
•	10 and under	60m	0.682m	10.5m	6.5m	10.5m	7	None	2.7kg
•	10 and under	60m	0.61m	10m	6m	14m	7	None	2.7kg

• In these age groups, the figures given are only suggestions. The only essentials are
(a) the distance; (b) the number of hurdles; (c) the height of the barriers. Spacings should
be adjusted to suit the individual and hurdles must be equally spaced.

The Technical Model (see figures 224, 225)

The dynamics of the whole model may be considered as three phases blending into each other in sequence.

Action at take-off

LEADING LEG	TRAILING LEG	TRUNK	ARMS
Picked up *well flexed* knee and hip; in line with the running action.	Vigorously extends to drive the athlete into the hurdle.	Square – but leaned into the lead leg thigh and barrier.	Leading elbow directed across hurdle – in line with normal running action. *Other wrist never further back than the hip.*
"FAST KNEE"	"DRIVE AT"	"DIP"	"REACH ACROSS"

Action across

Knee opens *naturally, never deliberately,* with the thought already of grounding the foot quickly.	The well flexed knee is pulled sharply to the arm pit (frog-like) – ankle cocked – heel in tight.	Shoulders and trunk balanced and square.	Leading *elbow* pulled *down* and *back*. Other arm *punched* through.
"UP-DOWN-FAST"	"KNEE HIGH:HEEL IN"	"PRESS FORWARD"	"FAST ARMS"

Action off/from

Leg strikes back and down – with the feeling of pushing the hip into the next stride.	Knee – still flexed, is pulled across the chest – heel still in tight.	Lean off the hurdle into the sprint.	Arms move into vigorous 'sprinting'.
"STRIKE THE GROUND AWAY"	"PULL ACROSS"	"LEAN INTO SPRINT"	"SPRINTING ARMS"

The whole action must be as horizontally directed as possible, with the emphasis on a fast, bent lead leg, and a high bent trailing leg. Looked at from the front, the leading leg should be moved *only* in the plane of running; the trailing heel should move only in the plane of running, and the shoulders should always be square to the plane of running.

Development of Leading Leg Action

From the onset of using 'drills' – the emphasis is on *speed of limb movement*. The pattern of most exercises is that the athlete jogs or prances – then executes the lead action at much higher speed than the preceding jog/prance.

The lead leg action is introduced as the fast high lift of the thigh, with knee well-flexed; followed by the rapid return of the foot to its starting point (figure 209a).

The movement is now executed whilst jogging on the spot – then whilst jogging forwards.

The next stage of development is to jog down the side of obstacles or hurdles, executing the fast lead leg movement over each obstacle (figure 209b). As the obstacle increases in height, the athlete attempts to 'run high' – picking up the lead knee higher and faster. *Always – the hip must press at the hurdle.*

A variation of this drill may be introduced. The athlete picks up the knee as before – but as it reaches its highest point, the athlete flicks the lower leg forwards, then swings the whole limb back and down, to return the foot to its starting point (209c). This drill helps in the movement 'off', or away from, the hurdle.

On running down the side of the hurdles – the athlete should be aware of the *first* drill movement, rather than the second, because I believe that the knee opens involuntarily in the full hurdling action – and it should not be coached as a voluntary act. The next progression is to perform these drills as part of the full action over the hurdle – but this cannot be done until the trail leg action has been developed. However, once the full action *is* employed, the coach must not only observe the action of the lead leg from the side – where the flexed knee and speed of action may be seen; but also from in front where the plane of action can be seen. If there is any deviation across the body or out from the body, the hurdle should be placed across a line, so that the athlete can focus his attention on keeping his knee down that line – and the coach can see the 'accuracy' of this action.

Development of Trail Leg Action

The trail leg action might be introduced as follows:-

(a)   The athlete turns his trail-foot outwards – à la Charlie Chaplin (figure (230).

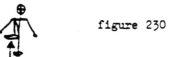

figure 230

(b)   He now pulls the trail knee up to his arm-pit. The knee is completely flexed, heel in tight.

(c)   The knee – still flexed, is pulled from the arm-pit to the middle of the chest.

(d)   The foot is now grounded.

(e)   This basic movement is now attempted over a low hurdle, with the athlete standing on his lead leg.

(f)   This is repeated with a walk – then a jog, into the movement.

(g)   Standing practices may be continued with higher barriers and with the athlete leaning over the hurdle – hands supported (figure 231).

figure 231

(h)   The athlete now introduces a trail leg drill down the side of hurdles, by performing a low lead leg action over a very low barrier, then snapping the trail leg over the hurdle. The shoulders *must* be kept square, and the athlete may ensure this by holding both arms forwards – as if holding the reins of a horse. Very quickly the *low* barrier may be removed.

(i)   The coach may observe the 'high knee – tight foot' from the side, or, from the front. However, the most important feature to watch for from the side, is that the heel is kept in tight (flexed knee), even when the knee is pulled across the chest. From the front, the coach will clearly see if the knee remains high as it comes across the chest, and that it only drops when the leg has assumed the normal plane of running. A hurdle across a line – as for lead leg – will help here, because a clue to the 'early' knee drop is the landing of the foot on the trail leg side of the line.

Trunk Position

I believe that for women's high hurdles and the 200 – 400 races, this point should not be laboured, due to the height of the barrier compared with the athlete's own height. However, for men's high hurdles, the athlete must learn to squeeze his chest *at* the hurdle – *onto* his lead thigh *fast*. This takes place *with the trail foot on the ground*! The sensation is of going *under* the hurdle. Aids such as dipping under a cane positioned above the hurdle have been used.

Arms

The lead arm (opposite lead leg) should be thought of as mimicking the down/back action of the lead leg, whilst making room for the advancing trail leg. Coaching comments such as 'wrists inside elbows', 'keep your arms sprinting' and so on, may help establish the movement for the athlete. Arm 'problems' usually arise through lack of balance – or through poor physical preparation. The balance problems are normally traceable to the leg movements – and compensatory rotation of the upper body (figure 232).

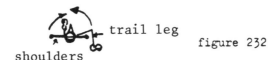

trail leg

figure 232

shoulders

Drills with shoulders kept square should help. For example, alternate trail leg action.

The Longer Hurdles Races

There are two unique problems in the longer races for hurdles.

1 Hurdling on a bend

2 Stride patterns

Hurdling on a bend

The left leg lead is preferred on the bend, not only because it helps the athlete hurdle 'into and with' the curve, but also because there is less chance of disqualification (figure 233).

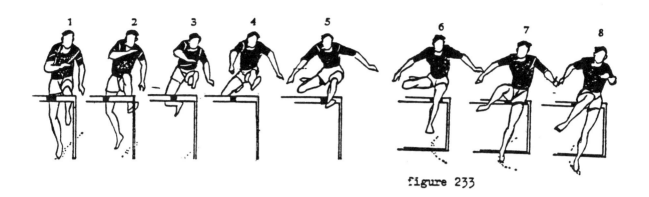

figure 233

The passage over the barrier on the bend should ensure that the athlete, on moving 'off' the hurdle, may hold the inside of his lane. This suggests moving to the middle of the lane prior to take-off (figure 234). Hurdling *must* be crisp.

figure 234

Stride patterns

If the athlete is to take every hurdle on the same leg, then there must be an odd number of strides between barriers, i.e. 7, 9, 11 for 200m, 13, 15, 17, 19 for 400m. If the athlete can hurdle on either leg, then even numbers of strides may be used, i.e. 8, 10, 12 for 200m, 12, 14,16, 18, 20 for 400m. It is normal for athletes to have a consistent number of strides between hurdles in 200m, e.g. 9 strides throughout; however, in 400m this is not normally the case. There *are* athletes who have run 13, 14, 15, 16 and 17 strides throughout – but if this happens, it would suggest that they are not using their full stride length between the earlier barriers. Most athletes need to 'change down' at one – or even two points in the race – a situation which demands spatial judgement, ability to regulate stride length, and planning. Clearly, it is better if the athlete can hurdle on either leg – as this will enable him to 'change down' gradually, e.g. 15 strides to hurdle 6; 16 strides to hurdle 8; 17 strides to finish. If this is not possible, the athlete must clip his strides quite severely, e.g. 15 strides to hurdle 6; 17 strides to finish. Between hurdles 6 and 7, he must clip his strides around the middle of 35m spacing (say strides 6,7,8,9) – avoiding adjustments into or off the hurdle.

It is useful to have the athlete count his strides between barriers, to accustom him to the rhythm.

I would emphasise here the importance of teaching the athlete to hurdle with either leg. In fact, one school of thought suggests that the athlete should learn to hurdle with either leg when he is introduced to the event.

Starting

In the high hurdles events, the athlete is attempting to reach top speed around hurdle 3, which means that the start is very much that of a sprinter. However, he must not still be rising at the first hurdle, which means that he is upright much earlier than the sprinter.

If an ODD number of strides are required to the first hurdle, the LEAD leg is in the FRONT block.

Conditioning

The hurdler requires the training of a sprinter, 200m, 400m – against a sound general background of fitness. The technical model will suggest *many* special exercises to the coach, and the following may help augment his armoury of such practices. (figures 235 – 294)

MIDDLE AND LONG DISTANCE

The distance events are those which make high endurance demands of the athlete. Whereas the contest between athletes over 60m is technique, speed and strength dependent, there is a progressive involvement of endurance dependence with increasing distance, or, to put it another way, with increasing duration of run.

Fuel

The energy required to move limbs is derived from our 'fuel'. The fuel comes in the first instance from the food we eat – but it is broken down to the more useable fuels of GLYCOGEN (like glucose) and FREE FATTY ACIDS. The analogy is of breaking down North Sea Oil to 5 Star and 3 Star petrol! The fuel is carried from the digestive system to storage or circulation, by the blood.

Oxygen

As with other fuels, it burns better with oxygen available. The oxygen is transported with the fuel to the engine (muscle) via the blood. The blood collects its oxygen from the lungs, and is pumped round the elaborate system of blood vessels linking lungs and working muscle, by the heart. The total system is called the OXYGEN TRANSPORTING SYSTEM or CARDIO-RESPIRATORY SYSTEM – or CARDIO VASCULAR SYSTEM. However, not only does it transport oxygen from the lungs to muscle, it also transports waste – the fuel's ashes – back to the lungs, liver or excretory systems to be recycled or passed out of the body.

3 Energy Pathways

The outcome of burning the FUEL is a substance called A.T.P. (A + P + P + P). Whenever a 'P' is split from the substance, energy is released – the energy which the muscle requires to contract. Chemical energy is thus converted to mechanical energy.

$$A + \begin{matrix} P \\ P \\ P \end{matrix} \quad \rightarrow \quad A + \begin{matrix} P \\ P \\ P \end{matrix} + ENERGY$$

(a) There are three 'pathways' for delivery of A.T.P. The oxygen transporting system ensures a supply of oxygen and fuel. The provision of A.T.P. can only be ensured here for as long as this supply lasts. For this reason, this energy pathway is called AEROBIC (*with oxygen*).

FUEL + OXYGEN → A.T.P. + WASTE (easily disposed of)

If this was the only means of making A.T.P., then clearly there would be no energy available to the muscle if fuel or oxygen 'run out'. Provided the rate of oxygen consumption is equal to the rate of provision – then the aerobic pathway can operate until fuel runs out. This is the problem facing a marathon or longer distance athlete. He must have extra supplies of fuel as the race proceeds, in the form of glucose drinks. He must also, incidentally, take a mixture of water and salts to replace fluid and salts lost through perspiration.

(b) It is, of course, quite likely that the athlete can be running so hard, that the body's oxygen needs exceed its rate of provision. In these circumstances, A.T.P. may still be formed, but the waste products cannot be disposed of.

BLOOD TRANSPORTED FUEL → A.T.P. + WASTE   (LACTIC ACID UNABLE TO BE DISPOSED OF)

Obviously, this situation can only exist for a limited period of time – after which activity ceases completely, the waste is flushed away, and the oxygen debt brought on by spending more than was available is repaid. This pathway is *without oxygen* and its title is ANAEROBIC. However, because this indiposable waste is LACTIC ACID, it is more aptly referred to as the LACTIC ANAEROBIC PATHWAY. This pathway is exhausted after approximately 45 seconds.

(c) The muscle, in fact, stores an energy fuel which, for simplicity I'll refer to as a P reservoir. When

$$\begin{matrix} P \\ + \\ A + P \\ + \\ P \end{matrix} \quad \rightarrow \quad \begin{matrix} P \\ A + P \\ + \\ P \end{matrix}$$

this reservoir can be tapped to replace the missing P. This can continue for as long as there are P's in the reservoir – roughly 15 seconds. Then one of the other two pathways must be employed. Again, there is no oxygen, so it is an ANAEROBIC – but nor is there waste – so this pathway is called the ALACTIC ANAEROBIC PATHWAY.

To summarise –

1 We must make A.T.P. available
2 It can be made by
   (a)   AEROBIC PATHWAY   (exhausted when fuel runs out)
   (b)   LACTIC ANAEROBIC PATHWAY   (exhausted after 45 seconds)
   (c)   ALACTIC ANAEROBIC PATHWAY   (exhausted after 15 seconds)

Endurance Events

The short distance sprinter – 60m – 200m must consider the possibility of almost completely anaerobic work. However, the 400m → MARATHON have a changing emphasis from great anaerobic, little aerobic work (400m – 800m) to little anaerobic, great aerobic (10,000m – marathon). Thus we have some authorities referring to

SHORT ENDURANCE EVENTS   (mainly anaerobic)
MEDIUM ENDURANCE EVENTS   (aerobic and anaerobic)
LONG ENDURANCE EVENTS   (predominantly aerobic)

It seems reasonable to assume that the emphasis on anaerobic work should be greater, where the anaerobic demands are higher. However, it must be emphasised that aerobic work is the foundation of all endurance events.

Types of Endurance

Endurance factors have certain implications for those mechanisms which eventually convert the chemical energy of the body's fuels to the mechanical energy required for moving the limbs with strength and speed, and maintaining such movement.

It may help an understanding of these implications if you consider certain types of endurance.

Speed Endurance

Speed endurance is the type of endurance where speed of limb movement is involved. It is clearly of greatest importance to the sprinter – and we believe that practices which encourage technical exactness in coordination, rhythm of movement, and relaxation, in the presence of endurance factors, help develop speed endurance.

Strength Endurance

Strength endurance is the type of endurance where strength or force of limb movement is involved. This type of endurance is of greatest importance from 400m through to Steeplechase, but seems to have most relevance to 800m. All resisted running actions are geared to the development of strength endurance. Thus sand running, harness running, short interval running, exaggerated action running, weights jacket running, hill running, etc., are intended to develop strength endurance.

Heart Endurance

Heart Endurance is in fact aerobic endurance – whereas speed and strength endurance are anaerobic endurance. Lactic involvement is heaviest in strength endurance.

It may serve as a reasonable rule of thumb, that if the athlete is running continuously with a heart rate of 140 – 160, he is running aerobically. If the heart rate moves up towards 170 – 190 and the work is continued beyond 30 – 40 seconds, he will be working anaerobically.

Although I've taken some time over the fuelling and oxygen transporting aspects of endurance running, obviously other factors will, from time to time, affect heart rate, performance capacity, and so on. Thus, the coach must consider the fluid balance systems (cooling systems) when high temperatures must be experienced, and so on. Most important, is that if there is any evidence of viral infections – even simple infections such as the common cold – THE ATHLETE MUST NOT TRAIN UNTIL GIVEN MEDICAL CLEARANCE TO DO SO.

Training

The types of endurance method may be classified as per figure 295.

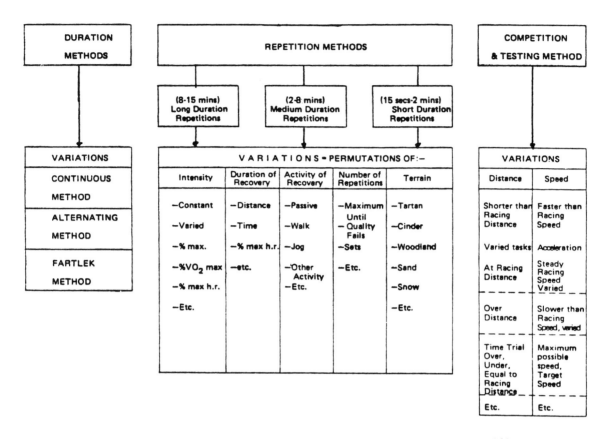

figure 295

In the development of the endurance athlete, the following stages should be followed:-

(a) A sound general strength and mobility basis (e.g. circuits, etc.).

(b) Development of a technically sound running action (e.g. teach athlete a model similar to the sprinting model – over 50m – 100m).

(c) Develop a sound aerobic basis – from interval runs to continuous runs, to alternating and fartlek runs. This order of things helps the coach educate the athlete in *pace judgement.*

(d) Develop strength endurance.

(e) Develop speed, speed endurance and specific endurance characteristics.

(f) Develop racing ability, tactics and so on.

Year Plans

October – mid-March	Aerobic Training, General Strength and Mobility, Running Technique, Cross Country races.
Mid-March – April	Strength Endurance, Aerobic Training.
May – mid-June	Speed Endurance, Speed, Special Endurance, Aerobic Endurance, Trials.
Mid-June – August	Competitions, Speed, Special Endurance, Aerobic Endurance.

The extent of running is, then, gradually progressed from October to March – then gently reduced as the intensity of training is increased to a high point in early June. There should be an oscillation between high and low intensity from June – August, according to the demands of competition.

Moreover, within a 28 day cycle, the athlete may operate a shift from easy long work, to harder shorter work from the first half to the second half of the cycle. Again, it is worth observing a policy of a harder day followed by an easier day, at all times.

Dietary supplements such as Vitamin B 12, Vitamin C, iron and so on, are very valuable to the endurance athlete, but it is worth seeking medical advice to monitor their intake.

STEEPLECHASE

The Steeplechaser is a distance athlete and, at the same time, an endurance hurdler. The hurdling action should be considered by the steeplechaser – but in addition to the normal barriers, which are *very* much heavier than normal hurdles, there is also a water jump (figure 296).

figure 296

Development of water jump may commence with leaping onto and from boxes, 3ft. diameter heavy logs and so on. The object here is to *stay close* to the barrier – springing out and across the water, rather than up and over.

The steeplechaser must be a strong and tenacious distance runner with a large background of strength endurance. Cross country racing is a sound basis for development of the 'chaser's' strength endurance.

Training for the steeplechase athlete *must* include elastic strength work – and should require multiple hurdle clearances in repetition runs.

RELAYS

Unlike other athletics disciplines, the relay is a team event. As such, it requires the cooperation of every team member for development of its technical component. Unfortunately, this fact is seldom appreciated by athletes – or indeed by selectors. Athletes often see the event as secondary in importance to their own individual events, while selectors seldom select a team, but rather draw together four athletes selected for other events. The danger of such an approach, is that the athletes and selectors do not appreciate that the amount of time spent on development of the technical component of the relay, should be equal to that for individual events.

The orthodox relays are 4 x 100m, and 4 x 400m, however there is an infinite number of variations. For example, there are shuttle hurdles relays, road relays, paarlaufs, 4 x 200m, 800, etc., Swedish relays, medley relays and so on.

The 4 x 100m relay is recognised as requiring considerable time on technical practice of change-overs, but the coach must not neglect the 4 x 400m changes – and their particular problems.

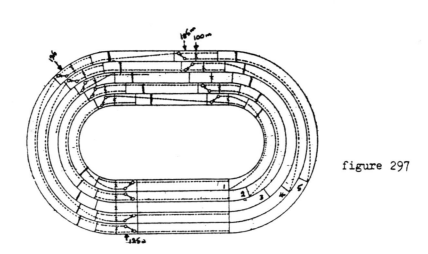

figure 297

4 x 100m

The athletes do not, in fact, run only 100m (figure 297). The first athlete, who must be a good starter and bend runner, must run approximately 105m; the second runner, who must be strong in the straight – and who must, more often than not, run into a headwind, must run approximately 125m; and the third runner, who must be a good bend runner, must run approximately 125m, while the last runner must be a powerful and aggressive finisher who can run with control and confidence for 120m.

These statistics are based on the baton being passed 5m from the end of the box at each change-over.

In order to ensure that the bend runners can run on the inside of the lane, they carry the baton in their right hand. To avoid time wastage through inefficient running, the athletes should not have to change hands. Putting these two requirements together, it is suggested that runner 1 carries the baton in his right hand; runner 2 in his left; runner 3 in his right; and runner 4 in his left (figure 297 – lane 2).

The object in all relay races where a baton is used, is to ensure that baton speed is not lost throughout the run. This means that the outgoing runner must already be moving before he receives the baton. More than this – he must be moving as fast as possible by the end of the 25 metres at his disposal (i.e. by the theoretical hand-over point 5 metres from the end of the zone).

For this to be possible, the outgoing runner measures out a check mark in foot lengths (his own feet). When the incoming runner's hips reach this mark, the outgoing runner begins to sprint away from the incoming runner. The incoming runner calls 'hand' when he thinks he can effect a change-over. This should be approximately in the middle of the box – with the change-over completed 5m later. The change-over can be thought of as successful *only* if neither outgoing nor incoming runner has to reduce speed to effect the change-over. The incoming runner should only *just* reach the outgoing runner by change-over. If the incoming athlete reaches the outgoing runner too early, then the check mark must be taken *out* (i.e. a greater distance). If the incoming runner fails to reach the outgoing runner, then the check mark must be taken *in*. These adjustments are all very well if the outgoing runner moves at the same speed every time – and on cue! – and if the incoming runner always comes in at the same speed. These factors can only be guaranteed, given sprinting fitness in both athletes, and the ability of the outgoing runner to sprint start on a visual cue. Practices such as sprinting when a tennis ball is rolled over a mark may help develop this ability.

figure 298   figure 299

The actual change-over must, then, be consistent, and given that the athletes *are* well trained sprinters, and that they *can* sprint on a visual cue, there are only two other factors to be considered. The first is the method of passing the baton. This can either be upsweep (figure 298) or downsweep (figure 299).

Whichever method is used, the same method must always be rehearsed. There is little to choose between the methods, but U.K. teams use upsweep. The athlete must learn to hold the hand steady, when it is called for, and offer a large target for the incoming runner (figure 299).

The second factor is that the method of starting must also be consistent. The starting position, whether standing, or a modified crouch, must allow the athlete a clear view of the check mark *and* a fast start. The first runner has a number of methods of holding the baton at the start from which to choose (figure 300).

figure 300

4 x 400m

The first bend, lap, or 500m may be in lanes, and the coach should ensure that the team knows which conditions apply!

Although tactical demands may dictate otherwise, it is usually sound to place the fastest athlete 4th, second fastest 1st, least experienced 2nd, and the other athlete 3rd. Avoid at all costs 'losing contact' with the opposition.

The baton is best taken in the right, then changed to the left. The outgoing runner should be aware of the fatigued state of the incoming runner, and, bearing this in mind, take the baton 'on the burst' – so that he can pick up a fast running rhythm on the first bend. Wherever possible, the change should be non-visual, but there is little or no case for check marks. When awaiting the incoming runner, the outgoing runner should ensure that he has ample space to receive the baton.

The athlete must learn to run on his own strengths for his leg of the relay, and *not* be lured into the opponent's race!

The relays are, as stated earlier, *team events,* and like other team games, the team must work and think *as a team*. The need for regular practices should, then be self evident. The coach must ensure that practices are conducted with athletes running the whole distance, once the basic check marks, etc. have been established. Competitions are a most valuable form of training in this respect.

WALKING

figure 301

Although most certainly a technical event, I believe that walking requires less contrived modification to the natural movement, than any other technical event. However, just as with running, there are *many* variations of perambulation – and it is well that time is spent very early in the athlete's development, to teach him an efficient technical model. The model is very tightly dictated by the rules, which state:-

"Race Walking is a progression of steps, so taken that unbroken contact with the ground is maintained. (1) During the period of each step, the advancing foot of the walker must make contact with the ground before the rear foot leaves the ground. (2) The supporting leg must be straightened (i.e. not bent at the knee) for at least one moment when in the vertical upright position."

Whilst this clumsy piece of wording sounds almost incapable of interpretation into actual movement, I believe that at the basic level, the athlete should simply concentrate on maintaining contact with the ground.

When establishing the technical model, the coach should focus the athlete's attention on:-

The feet:
The athlete's feet should be placed along a straight line (figure 302) – Charlie Chaplin had trouble with this technique! The emphasis, then, is on placing the inside of the heel on the ground, and walking along the inside edge of the shoe, along the line of progression. Walking along a painted line is useful here. The athlete should use the whole foot – and feel that he has pushed off the ball/toes of one foot – onto the heel of the other.

figure 302

Knees:

I believe that the knee will straighten quite naturally when the supporting leg reaches the vertical. What is more important is that it is straightened vigorously as the leg pushes the athlete onto the other foot. The general impression here is of an extension at hip, knee, ankle – with a push off the ball/toes of the foot.

Hips:

The hip action is possibly the most complex. The need for swinging the hip forward is well explained by figure 303. It enhances stride length. At the same time the hip should describe a wave-like motion, reaching

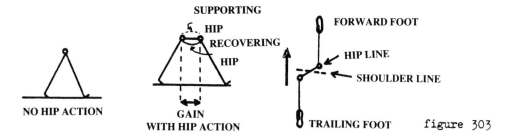

figure 303

a high point when the supporting leg is straightened in the vertical position, and a low point during recovery, when it passes the straightened leg (figure 301). This helps avoid a total rise and fall of the body. This can be practised, with the knee and foot actions on the spot – then introducing forward progression.

The trunk:

The back and abdominal muscles must be strong, because there is considerable involvement of these groups in maintaining a strong, erect posture. The back must be straight – but not tensed.

The shoulders/arms:

In order to avoid unnecessary energy/expenditure due to adverse rotations transferred to the trunk from the legs/hips – a powerful arm action should be used. This is not unlike the sprint arm action, in that it is over a wide range, and the elbows are maintained as near as possible at 90° flexion. The elbow should be pulled high behind the body, and the arms should swing across in front of the body (figure 304). Shoulders should be kept square to the direction of movement – but again, not tense.

The head:

This should not be allowed to roll about at any point in the race.

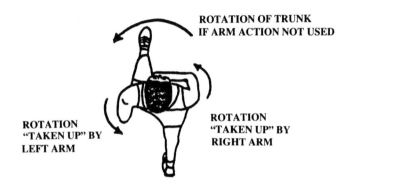

figure 304

Eyes should be fixed forward, head steady, but neck muscles must not be tensed.

Conditioning

The importance of a sound basic level of strength cannot be over-emphasised. Moreover, hip mobility should be emphasised in mobility programmes. I suggest that development against this background should be:-

(a) Develop general endurance in running, skiing, etc.

(b) Teach athletes basics of technique – and perform interval training type walks along lines at a speed which allows sound technique to be maintained.

(c) Develop walking endurance via hill treks, road walks, track 'marathons', Thistle Jogging Scheme, etc.

(d) Introduce special walk training programmes along lines similar to running endurance (see middle/long distance), i.e. including strength work, strength endurance work and so on.

THE COMBINED EVENTS – HEPTATHLON AND DECATHLON

HEPTATHLON is to women as DECATHLON is to men, although there is, of course, a less popular men's pentathlon. The concept of a multi-discipline event dates back to the earliest Greek Olympics of the 8th Century B.C. This concept in many ways reflected the philosophy of the balanced personality, because not only was it thought right to balance physical with intellectual prowess, it was also thought right to balance the total physical being. In other words, this was the non-specialist era.

I would like to emphasise the concept of the multi-discipline event *as a single event,* and not as a group of individual events. The athlete should be encouraged to view Heptathlon and Decathlon in this light. Development then becomes one of:-

(a) Teaching the athlete the basic techniques involved against a sound basis of general strength, mobility and endurance.

(b) Making available Heptathlon/Decathlon competitions whilst developing the basic fitness factors already mentioned, plus speed.

(c) Concentrating on development of the weak events and on improvement of the poorer fitness factors.

(d) Using individual competitions to help develop both weak and strong events, as adjuncts to training.

(e) Progressing the level of Heptathlon/Decathlon Competitions.

Stage (c) of this suggested development is extremely important, because the athlete's overall multi-event score is more likely to improve by concentrating on strengthening the weak events.

HEPTATHLON

The Disciplines

DAY 1

100m Hurdles:

This is the keystone of the Heptathlon because training influences other events. This must be practised throughout the year, and the indoor season should be used.

High Jump:

Flop has helped the Heptathlon because it is easier than straddle to learn – and to record good heights early in development. This is the most generous points scoring event.

Shot Putt:

This is a critical event and traditionally our worst. Specific technique and strength work are essential.

200m:

Training for the 100m Hurdles serves the 200m well. The long day, splitting the two track events by the lengthy High Jump and Shot Putt suggests a thorough sprint warm-up for the 200m.

DAY 2

Long Jump:

Good hurdlers/long jumpers are successful in Heptathlon – for example the G.D.R. athletes Neubert (13.13/6.79m), Vater (13.38/6.76m) and Paetz (13.06/6.68m). As Heptathlon develops, it is anticipated that high scores will be built on the foundation of Long, High, 100H and 200m. Hitch kick and hitch hang are the most popular flight techniques.

Javelin:

Like the Shot Putt, this throw will normally score low. Added to this is the problem of Javelin being such a highly specialised event. Specific technique and strength work are essential.

800m:

This event is the most time demanding in terms of training – but yields disproportionate points return. Nevertheless, the heptathlete must look to an intelligent balance of aerobic and anaerobic training to ensure minimal points fall-off at the end of two hard days.

The disciplines are contested in the order given.

Only three trials are allowed in field events, which puts a unique stress on the athlete, but which helps to 'discipline' the athlete in the individual event.

The following table may help the coach gauge average performances in each event against possible totals.

TOTAL =	7000	6300	5600	4900	4200	3500
(Average per event)	(1000)	(900)	(800)	(700)	(600)	(500)
100H	13.6	14.3	15.1	15.9	16.7	17.6
High Jump	1.82	1.74	1.65	1.57	1.48	1.39
Shot Put	17.07	15.58	14.09	12.58	11.07	9.55
200m	23.6	24.6	25.7	26.9	28.2	29.5
Long Jump	6.48	6.16	5.84	5.50	5.15	4.78
Javelin	57.18	52.04	46.88	41.68	36.46	31.22
800m	2:07.63	2:14.52	2:21.77	2:29.47	2:37.70	2:46.60

Conditioning

Against the sound basis of general strength, mobility and endurance, the athlete must develop the technical and conditioning components of the individual disciplines, and at the same time develop the capacity to concentrate on each discipline as it arises in the competition – *and* endure the two day programme.

A possible training microcycle of 14 days in the winter may look like this.

1 Hurdles technique + rep. runs
2 Circuit/Stage training + Game
3 Javelin technique + Game
4 Rest
5 High Jump tech. + Circuit/Stage/Weights.
6 Shot technique + Game
8 Long Jump tech. + Sprint technique
9 Repetition runs
10 Circuit/Stage/Weights + Game
11 Rest
12 Triathlon (Run-Jump-Throw) or Day 1 events or Day 2 events plus 45 mins. steady run or Fartlek.
13 Circuit/Stage/Weights. + rep. runs
14 Rest

DECATHLON

The Disciplines

DAY 1

100m:

The two highest speed disciplines are first event each morning. Peak concentration must be assured to avoid dropping points unnecessarily.

Long Jump:

The 100m should be a good "warm-up" for Long Jump. Hitch and hitch hang are the most popular flight techniques. *Height* of jump must be emphasised.

Shot Putt:

A poor event for us normally, and quite divorced from other events on the first day. Technique and strength work are essential.

High Jump:

With Pole Vault, has shown the greatest improvement at international level. Flop has helped a great deal.

400m:

We normally score well here because of hard workouts throughout the year.

DAY 2

110m Hurdles:

Hurdles training and technique help all other disciplines, and the athlete should work on this event throughout the year.

Discus:

Like shot – not normally a high point scorer, but sound technique and strength improvement, reap considerable dividends.

Pole Vault:

Fibre-pole vaulting is essential, and the athlete should work hard on this highly technical event. Indoor competition should be used.

Javelin:

As with the other two throws – not a good point scorer – mainly because javelin 'arms' are hard to come by! Again, technique and strength work *will* improve scoring potential.

1500m:

Universally the worst event, but one where simply time spent running in training will give quick returns.

The disciplines are contested in the order given.

The first day is clearly less technical than the second – and this in some way explains why on the one hand the greatest improvements at international level have come from increasing the second day scores; whilst at grass roots level, the second day's points are roughly 20% – 25% less than the first day's points. Concentration on strength and on technique is a sound investment of time.

The two days may also be thought of as the jump day and the throws day.

As with heptathlon, the emphasis must be on strengthening the weak events in training.

The following table may help the coach gauge average performance in each event against possible totals.

	POINTS									
TOTAL =	8000	7500	7000	6500	6000	5500	5000	4500	4000	3500
(Av/Event)	(800)	(750)	(700)	(650)	(600)	(550)	(500)	(450)	(400)	(350)
100m	11.0	11.3	11.5	11.8	12.0	12.3	12.6	12.9	13.2	13.5
Long Jump	6.94	6.73	6.51	6.29	6.06	5.83	5.59	5.34	5.09	4.83
Shot Put	15.16	14.35	13.53	12.71	11.89	11.07	10.24	9.40	8.56	7.72
High Jump	2.00	1.94	1.88	1.83	1.77	1.71	1.64	1.58	1.51	1.45
400m	50.2	51.3	52.4	53.6	54.8	56.1	57.4	58.8	60.2	61.8
110mH	15.2	15.6	16.1	16.5	17.0	17.5	18.0	18.6	19.1	19.7
Discus	46.60	44.16	41.72	39.26	36.80	34.30	31.78	29.24	26.68	24.10
Pole Vault	4.63	4.47	4.29	4.12	3.94	3.76	3.57	3.38	3.18	2.97
Javelin	64.10	60.78	57.46	54.12	50.74	47.36	43.96	40.52	37.06	33.56
1500m	4:21.77	4:29.25	4:36.96	4:44.94	4:53.20	5:01.78	5:10.73	5:20.10	5:29.96	5:40.41

Conditioning

Clearly, this athlete must have a very sound all-round strength, plus mental and physical endurance as a basis to development. On this base, he must develop the technical and conditioning components of each discipline, at the same time developing the capacity to concentrate on each discipline as it arises – and the two hard days of competition. Throughout the winter, he should use indoor competition wherever possible – even attempting indoor pentathlon, etc.

A possible training microcycle of 14 days in the winter, may look like this:-

1	Hurdles Technique + running technique	8	Active or passive recovery
2	Weakest Jump + special strength	9	Discus + repetition runs + special strength
3	Weakest throw + general strength	10	Pole vault + general strength
4	Active or passive recovery	11	Javelin + fartlek/steady run
5	Long Jump + sprinting + special strength	12	Active or passive recovery
6	Shot + repetition runs	13	Triathlon (or weakest event) + repetition runs
7	High Jump + general strength	14	Passive rest

GENERAL BASIC CONDITIONING

We assume a great deal when the athlete is introduced to the various technical and energy demands of track and field events. For example, amongst other things, we assume –

Strength:

i.e. that the athlete is strong enough to meet the technical requirements of the event – not only in the dynamic elements such as the jumping leg or throwing arm, but also in the static or postural elements such as the 'strong back' in jumping.

Mobility:

i.e. that the athlete has sufficient range of movement in his joints to meet the technical requirements of the event.

Endurance:

i.e. that the athlete has sufficient stamina to repeat practices many times (repetition is the mother of learning!).

A sound basic conditioning in strength, mobility and endurance should ensure that errors of technique do not arise due to compensation for deficiency in these areas. Clearly, different events require varying degrees of development of these areas. For example, endurance is critical to middle distance events, while strength is more important in the throws. Nevertheless, *all* athletes should be *athletic* – and consequently should have a background of work in all these areas. It has been suggested that SPEED also should be included as a basic element of general conditioning, but I believe that it is so specific to the technical model of a given event, that it does not have a general application. Suffice it to be said here that speed is fundamentally the product of rhythm, coordination and relaxation, and should be developed as a sophisticated form of technique. Technique must never be sacrificed for speed.

The basic conditioning areas may be developed along the following lines:-

(a) **Strength**

This may be introduced via the school P.E. programme in general activity units, where a selection of exercises drawn from those listed below is used.

The next step is to bring in a more ordered approach via circuit training. Numbers of repetitions for each exercise should be determined as follows:-

   i   Determine *maximum* repetitions for arm exercises = M
   ii   Determine *maximum* repetitions in 60 seconds for leg and trunk exercises = M
   iii Divide M by 2 = $\frac{M}{2}$ = T
   iv   In each circuit, the athlete does 'T' repetitions for the relevant exercise.
   v   The training unit = 3 circuits with 2 minutes between each circuit.

When the athlete does his first unit he will record a time of say 25 mins for the complete unit. When this time is reduced by 20% (20 mins.), he should then try 4, then 5 circuits for units. Once 5 circuits have been attempted 4 – 6 times, then the athlete should move from circuit to stage training.

In stage training, the athlete calculates $\frac{M}{3}$ = S, and the athlete does *all* of his sets of 'S' repetitions in a given exercise, one after the other, with 30 secs. between sets. He starts by doing 5 sets, then eventually progresses gradually to 10 sets. He also takes 30 secs. between exercises. This type of training is very sound for the development of *relative strength* (i.e. where body weight must be taken into consideration).

Where greater *absolute strength* is required, the athlete now moves to weight training, either as circuit or stage training – selecting exercises appropriate to the specific demands of his event. General and special exercises are listed below. The athlete *must* learn the technically correct method for executing each exercise, and work with light implements in 3 sets of 6 – 10 repetitions, before moving on to heavy weights.

(b) **Mobility**

This may again be introduced via the school Physical Education units, or special mobility units which are part of a club's early winter training programme. Gradually, however, the athlete will build into his warm-up a range of mobility exercises drawn from those listed here – or from others learned elsewhere: and the need for special units will be reduced.

Active mobility will always precede passive mobility which, in turn, will precede kinetic mobility – both in long term development, and within mobility units, warm-ups, and so on.

The role of mobility training may rest either in seeking a greater range of movement in specific joint actions, or simply in maintaining the existing range.

6 – 10 repetitions of each exercise should provide the necessary training effect, provided that coaches have ensured that each exercise is executed correctly.

(c) **Endurance**

This is originally developed naturally through games and the general activity of children and young people. It is progressed according to the nature of its requirement for various events, using the principles outlined in the *endurance events* section. In addition, however, the coach must consider the development of special throws endurance, jumps endurance and hurdles endurance via high repetitions of specific exercises. These "special" endurances form a specific strength-endurance base for high repetitions of techniques practices. Broadly speaking, the development of the athlete's fitness takes the following pattern:-

STAGE 1   DEVELOPMENT OF GENERAL FITNESS

STRENGTH	MOBILITY	ENDURANCE
Games	Games	Gynastics
Circuits	Gymnastics	Fartlek, Cross Country, etc.
Stage	Mobility Units	Repetition runs, circuits, etc.
Weights	Warm up	

STAGE 2   DEVELOPMENT OF BASIC TECHNIQUE

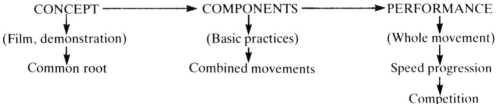

CONCEPT ⟶ COMPONENTS ⟶ PERFORMANCE

(Film, demonstration)   (Basic practices)   (Whole movement)

Common root   Combined movements   Speed progression

Competition

STAGE 3   DEVELOPMENT OF SPECIAL FITNESS

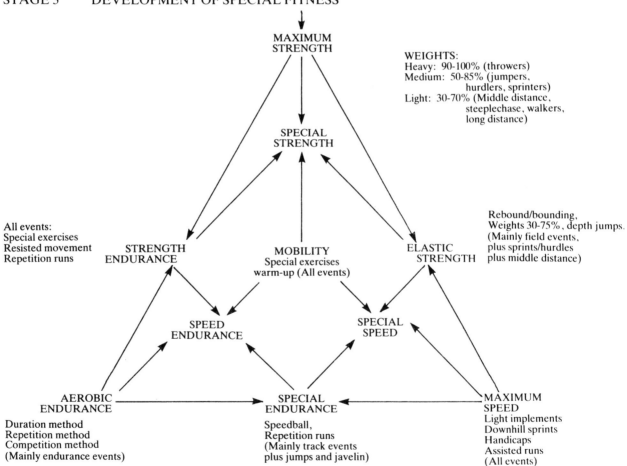

MAXIMUM STRENGTH

WEIGHTS:
Heavy: 90-100% (throwers)
Medium: 50-85% (jumpers, hurdlers, sprinters)
Light: 30-70% (Middle distance, steeplechase, walkers, long distance)

SPECIAL STRENGTH

All events:
Special exercises
Resisted movement
Repetition runs

STRENGTH ENDURANCE   MOBILITY Special exercises warm-up (All events)   ELASTIC STRENGTH

Rebound/bounding, Weights 30-75%, depth jumps. (Mainly field events, plus sprints/hurdles plus middle distance)

SPEED ENDURANCE   SPECIAL SPEED

AEROBIC ENDURANCE   SPECIAL ENDURANCE   MAXIMUM SPEED

Duration method
Repetition method
Competition method
(Mainly endurance events)

Speedball,
Repetition runs
(Mainly track events plus jumps and javelin)

Light implements
Downhill sprints
Handicaps
Assisted runs
(All events)

'Special' endurance/speed/strength require specialised exercises developed for a given event.

63

STAGE 4   DEVELOPMENT OF ADVANCED TECHNIQUE

Specialised practices and drills

PLANNING THE PROGRAMME

Broadly speaking, the year is divided as follows:

Months	Nov	Dec	Jan	Feb	Mar	Apr	May	Jun	Jul	Aug	Sep	Oct
Phases	1				2			3	4		5	6
Periods	PREPARATION						COMPETITION					TRANSITION

For the beginner athlete, Phase 1 might be represented as commencing with a 12 – week programme of all-event instruction to establish basic techniques. See page 65.

This might be followed in early Phase 2 by six weeks where 2 days are devoted to an elected event and related conditioning – and 1 day for rotation of elected other events. The rotation will be: week 1 – track event, week 2 – jump event, week 3 – throw event.

The weekly picture will now look as on page 66.

Planning development of the young athlete.

PHASE 1

	Week 1	2	3	4	5	6	7	8	9	10	11	12
TUESDAY	a. Sprint b. Mobility and circuit c. Repetition 100m	a. High Jump b. Mobility and circuit c. Repetition 100m	a. Javelin b. Mobility and circuit c. Repetition 100m	a. Hurdles b. Mobility and circuit c. Repetition 100m	a. Long Jump b. Stage c. Repetition 200m	a. Discus b. Stage c. Repetition 200m	a. Middle Dis. b. Stage c. Repetition 200m	a. Triple Jp.* b. Stage c. Repetition 200m	a_1. Shot Put b. Intro. Wts a_2. Relays	a_1. Walk b. Intro. Wts a_2. Relays	a. Pole Vault* b. Intro. Wts c. Relays	a. Hammer* b. Intro. Wts c. Relays
THURSDAY	a. Sprint b. Mobility and circuit c. Repetition 150m	a. High Jump b. Mobility and circuit c. Repetition 150m	a. Javelin b. Mobility and circuit c. Repetition 150m	a. Hurdles b. Mobility and circuit c. Repetition 150m	a. Long Jump b. Stage c. Repetition 120m	a. Discus b. Stage c. Repetition 120m	a. Middle Dis. b. Stage c. Repetition 100m	a. Triple Jp.* b. Stage c. Repetition 120m	a. Shot Put b. Intro. Wts c. Special repetitions	a. Walk b. Intro Wts c. Special repetitions	a. Pole Vault* b. Intro. Wts c. Special repetitions	a. Hammer* b. Intro. Wts c. Special repetitions
SATURDAY	a_1. Sprint a_2. General runs b. Cross country	a_1. High Jump a_2. General jumps b. Cross country	a_1. Javelin a_2. General throws b. Cross country	a_1. Hurdles a_2. General throws b. Cross country	a_1. Long Jump a_2. General jumps b. Cross country	a_1. Discus a_2. General throws b. Cross country	a_1. Sprint a_2. Elected event b. Special conditioning	a_1. Triple Jp.* a_2. Elected event b. Special conditioning *Long Jump for girls	a_1. Shot Put a_2. Elected event b. Special conditioning	a_1. Walk a_2. Elected event b. Special conditioning	a_1. Pole Vault* a_2. Elected event b. Special conditioning *High Jump for girls	a_1. Hammer* a_2. Elected event b. Special conditioning *Discus, Shot or Javelin for girls

In Phase 1, given a basis of general strength, mobility and endurance, the club athletes are given instruction in all events. Each training day sees a complex of 3 units (a technique unit (a, a_1, a_2) and two conditioning units (b, c). From week 6, the athlete may elect for an event for additional technical work on Saturdays, and with a growing knowledge of the athlete's status of fitness, the coach may devise special conditioning for the athlete – possibly related to his elected event. Relays are introduced in week 9 in terms of technical instruction – then are used as a conditioning method. Mobility, once introduced, is absorbed in unit "warm-ups". From week 9, Thursday's repetitions unit is over a distance specific to the athlete's needs.

In Phase 2, the 3-day pattern shifts for 6 weeks to 2 days on elected events and conditioning related to athlete and elected event; and 1 day on continued technical instruction on the basis of week 1 – elected track event; week 2 – elected jump; week 3 – elected throw, etc. – plus general conditioning. For the next 6 weeks, this pattern may be continued – or all 3 days may be devoted to the athlete's elected event and related conditioning.

Early Phase 2

Sprints and Hurdles

TUESDAY: (a)   Technique runs 2 – 3 x 3 – 5 x 30m – 90m
                  gradual increase in speed through Phase 1.
            (b)   General strength 3 x 6 – 10 x light weights.

THURSDAY: (a)   Special exercises – combining specific strength, mobility and coordination.
                  30 – 60 mins.
            (b)   Repetition runs 1 – 3 x 3 – 5 x 100m – 150m, good running technique throughout unit.

SATURDAY: (a)   2nd elected event technique.
            (b)   20 – 30 mins. special exercises for 2nd elected event.
            (c)   Repetition runs 1 – 2 x 3 – 6 x 200m – 300m.

        Note
          i   hurdles are used in the technique runs and special exercises for hurdlers.
          ii   400m athletes – their repetition runs are 1 – 2 x 3 – 6 x 300m on Saturdays.

Endurance Events (800m upwards, plus Steeplechase, Walks)

TUESDAY: (a)   General strength – stage or 3 – 6 x 10 light weights.
            (b)   30 mins. runs with alternating pace each 800m (H.R. 130 – 150/160 – 180)

THURSDAY: (a)   30 mins easy run (H.R. 130 – 150)
            (b)   30 – 45 mins paarlauf or continuous relay.

SATURDAY: (a)   2nd elected event technique.
            (b)   30 – 40 mins. fartlek or cross country.

        Note
          i   Steeplechase athletes may include hurdles in Thursday b.
          ii   Running technique must remain sound in Thursday b. The coach should look on
              this unit in terms of technique.
          iii Walks – Walk on Tuesday and Thursday, run on Saturday.
          iv All events will probably elaborate on the 3-day programme with at least one other
              day when the athlete runs 30 – 40 mins. easy (H.R. 130 – 150).

Jumps

TUESDAY: (a)   Technique training – standing, 1 – 5 step, short approach. Longer approach for
                  vaulters. (3 – 6 x 4 – 10 x practices). All aspects of jump/vault are worked on.
            (b)   General strength – 3 x 6 – 10 x light weights.

THURSDAY: (a)   Special exercises combining specific strength, mobility and coordination,
                  30 – 60 mins.
            (b)   Repetition runs – 1 – 3 x 3 – 5 x 100 – 150m. – good running technique
                  throughout unit.

SATURDAY: (a)   2nd elected event technique.
            (b)   20 – 30 mins. special exercises for 2nd elected event.
            (c)   Repetition runs 1 – 2 x 3 – 6 x 150 – 250m.

        Note
          i   Vaulters may also do technique training as part of special exercises.

Throws

TUESDAY: (a)   Technique training – standing, approach, isolation, partial techniques, etc.
                  (3 – 6 x 4 – 10 x practices).
            (b)   General strength – 3 – 5 x 3 – 8 x medium weights.

THURSDAY: (a)   Special exercises combining specific strength, mobility and coordination.
                  30 – 60 mins.
            (b)   Basketball or Volleyball or Squash, etc. 20 – 40 mins.

SATURDAY: (a)   2nd elected event technique.
            (b)   20 – 30 mins. special exercises for 2nd elected event.
            (c)   General strength as Tuesday b.

Phase 2 continued + Phase 4

Sprints and Hurdles

TUESDAY: (a)   Sprint speed 2 – 3 x 3 – 6 x 20m – 40m rolling start.

or

Start technique 1 – 2 x 4 – 6 x 30m – 40m

or

Acceleration 1 – 2 x 3 – 4 x 50m – 80m.

or

1 – 2 x 3 – 4 x 30m accelerate, 30m decelerate, 30m accelerate

or

etc.

        (b)   General strength 3 x 5 – 8 x medium weights.

THURSDAY: (a)   Special exercises – as before.

        (b)   Repetition runs 1 – 3 x 2 – 4 x 120m – 150m.

or

2 – 4 x (150 – 120 – 90m)

or

2 – 4 x (120 – 90 – 60m)

or

etc.

SATURDAY: (a)   2nd elected event technique.

        (b)   Sprint technique or 20 mins special exercises for 2nd elected event.

        (c)   Repetition runs 1 – 2 x 2 – 4 x 200 – 300m

or

100 – 200 – 300 – 200 – 100m

or

300 – 250 – 200 – 150 – 100m

or

etc.

Note

i   Hurdlers use hurdles wherever possible e.g. Saturday 'b', etc.

ii   400m athletes – Thursday b.   1 – 3 x 3 – 5 x 120 – 200m.

or

3 – 5 x (180 – 150 – 120m)

or

3 – 5 x (150 – 120 – 150m)

or

etc.

Saturday c.   2 – 3 x 2 – 4 x 300 – 500m

or

250 – 350 – 450 – 350 – 250m

or

600 – 500 – 400 – 300 – 200 – 100m

or

etc.

iii   Hurdlers use runs over sections of the 'race' – e.g. 200m hurdles and 300m hurdles for 400m hurdler; 3 hurdles, 5 hurdles, 7 hurdles for 'high' hurdler. These are built into repetition runs or technique runs or special exercises.

Endurance Events (800m upwards, plus Steeplechase plus Walks)

TUESDAY: (a)   General strength – stage or 2 – 4 x 10 – 15 x light weights.

        (b)   45 mins run with alternating pace each 1km (H.R. 130 – 150/160 – 180).

THURSDAY: (a)   30 mins easy run.

        (b)   Repetition runs – 1 – 4 x 2 – 5 x 300m – 1,000m.

or

2 – 4 x (600 – 400 – 300 – 200 – 100m).

or

etc.

SATURDAY (a) 30 mins easy run.
or
Interval training.
(b) 45 mins Fartlek with 10 – 12 hills of 100 – 200m.
or
Cross country.

Note
i Steeplechase athletes should work over hurdles on track units – and should also work technique over the water jump.
ii Walkers walk on Tuesday and Thursdays – run on Saturdays.
iii All events will probably elaborate on the 3-day programme with at least one other day where the athlete runs 30 – 45 mins easy (H.R. 130 – 150).

Jumps

TUESDAY: (a) Technique training – progressive intensity (increase in strength and speed).
Long/Triple
3 – 6 x 4 – 10 x 7 – 15 stride jumps
– rolling starts used in pursuit of less fatigue per unit.
or
High speed 'touch-off' jumps used in alternate sets with short approach maximum height jumps, 4 – 6 x 4 – 6 alternating.
or
etc.
Pole Vault
3 – 6 x 4 – 6 light pole short approach vaults.
or
3 – 4 x 3 – 5 x alternating light and normal pole; medium – full approach vault.
or
etc.
High Jump
3 – 6 x 4 – 10 x 3 – 5 stride approach.
or
4 – 6 x 4 – 6 x alternate full and short approach.
or
etc.
(b) General strength – 3 x 5 – 8 x medium weights.
THURSDAY: (a) Special exercises – as before with progressing intensity.
(c) Repetition runs – 1 – 3 x 2 – 4 x 120 – 150m.
or
2 – 4 x (150 – 120 – 90m).
or
2 – 4 x (120 – 90 – 60m).
or
etc.
SATURDAY: (a) 2nd elected technique.
(b) Sprint speed 2 – 3 x 3 – 4 x 20 – 40m rolling start.
or
Acceleration 2 – 3 x 3 – 4 x 40m standing start.
(c) Repetition runs – 1 – 2 x 2 – 4 x 150 – 200m.
or
1 – 2 x 2 – 4 x 40m sprint – 40m decelerate – 40m sprint.
or
2 – 4 x 2 – 4 x 50m stride – 50m sprint.

Note
i Due to the complexity of vaulting technique, the vaulter may vault on Saturday rather than work on his 2nd elected event; and on Thursday as part of his special exercises.

Throws

TUESDAY: (a) Technique training – progressive intensity (increase in strength and speed).
Isolation, partial technique, full throws (short approach 3 – 5 stride – plus full

approach Javelin) with varying weight of implement (both heavier and lighter by no more than 20%).

3 – 6 x 4 – 10 x practices – normal implement – partial or full throw.

or

4 – 6 x 4 – 6 x alternating weight of implement.

or

4 – 6 x 4 – 6 x alternating with/without weights jacket (5% body weight).

or

etc.

	(b)	General strength – 3 – 5 x 2 – 5 x heavy weights.
THURSDAY:	(a)	Special exercises as before.
	(b)	Sprints – 3 – 4 x 3 – 4 x 20m from blocks.

or

Game – basketball, football, tennis, etc.

SATURDAY:	(a)	2nd elected event technique.
	(b)	20 mins special exercises for 2nd elected event or for 'main' event.
	(c)	General strength – as for Tuesday b.

The picture changes again in Phase 3/5 to bring the athlete to readiness for frequent competition.

Phase 3/5

Sprints/Hurdles

| TUESDAY: | (a) | Technique practices as required, including relays practice. |
| | (b) | Special endurance (Speed) |

2 – 3 x full recovery runs over racing distance + 20% (100, 200 High Hurdles).

or

3 – 4 x full recovery runs over 350m or 300m or 250m (400m and low/intermediate hurdles).

or

2 – 3 x full recovery special task runs e.g. 300m at 90% racing pace – then as fast as possible for 150m (400m and 400 Hurdles).

or

2 – 3 x full recovery sub-maximum runs over 300m (100, 200m) or 500m (400m and 400 Hurdles).

or

etc.

| THURSDAY: | (a) | Special exercises and drills for speed and elastic strength. |
| | (b) | Sprint speed |

2 – 3 x 3 – 4 x 20 – 60m from blocks (100m, 200m, High Hurdles).

or

2 – 3 x 3 – 4 x 20 – 40m rolling (100, 200m, High Hurdles).

or

2 – 4 x 150 – 250m from blocks (400m and 400 Hurdles).

or

etc.

| SATURDAY: | | Competition |

or

| (a) | Technique practices as required. |
| (b) | 6 – 12 x 150m stride, 250m walk recovery. |

Note

i   Hurdlers will use hurdles in most sprint practices. When 'rolling start' work is used, the hurdles may be brought slightly closer to simulate the 'late race' situation in high hurdles. The 400m hurdler may work on stride change-downs on Tuesdays.

Endurance Events

| TUESDAY: | (a) | 30 mins easy run |
| | (b) | Repetition runs – 1 – 4 x 2 – 4 x 300 – 600m. |

or

2 – 3 x (600 – 400 – 300 – 200 – 100).

or

3 – 6 x differential 400's (i.e. first 200m at 80% racing speed, second 200m as fast as possible).

THURSDAY: (a) 30 – 45 mins easy run
           (b) Repetition runs 2 – 3 x 3 – 6 x 150m.
                or
                2 – 4 x 3 – 8 x 100m.
                or
                clock-work – 30 – 50 – 70 – 90 – 110 – 130 – 150m – then back down the 'clock'.
                or
                etc.
SATURDAY: Competition

Note
i   Steeplechasers will use hurdles on the Tuesday.
ii Walkers will use 2 x 30 mins on Tuesday and use Tuesday's repetition distances (or longer) on Thursday, following 45 mins walk.

Jumps

TUESDAY: (a) Technique practices as required – including relay practice.
           (b) 4 – 8 x 40m from standing.
                3 – 6 x 150m fast and relaxed.
THURSDAY: (a) 4 – 6 x approach runs.
           (b) Short or full approach jumps as required.
           (c) 2 – 4 x 3 – 4 x 20 – 30m rolling – if athlete requires sharpness.
                or
                4 – 8 x 120m fast stride – if the athlete requires to loosen off.
SATURDAY: Competition
                or
           (a) Special exercises as before – emphasising speed.
           (b) 6 – 12 x 150m stride, 250m walk.

Note
When there is no competition, the vaulter may choose to vault in training instead of Saturday a.

Throws

TUESDAY: (a) Technique practices as required.
           (b) General strength – 3 x 5 – 8 x medium weights – light weights.
THURSDAY: (a) 3 – 12 x throws as required using weight equal to or lighter than competition weight.
           (b) Selected special exercises – emphasising speed.
           (c) 4 – 6 x 20m sprints.
SATURDAY: Competition
                or
           (a) Technique practices as required.
           (b) General strength as Tuesday b.

It must be clearly understood that these are only *suggested* programmes and that coaches will modify this in the course of a Phase. Eventually, for the beginner athlete, the policy must be one of unbiased development, while preparing him to compete well in his 'main' event. Some beginner athletes will be able to train more than three times per week. If so, it is better to advance the athlete's technique in his second (or third) elected event, or his broad conditioning programme, rather than focus too much concentration on the specifics of his first elected (main) event.

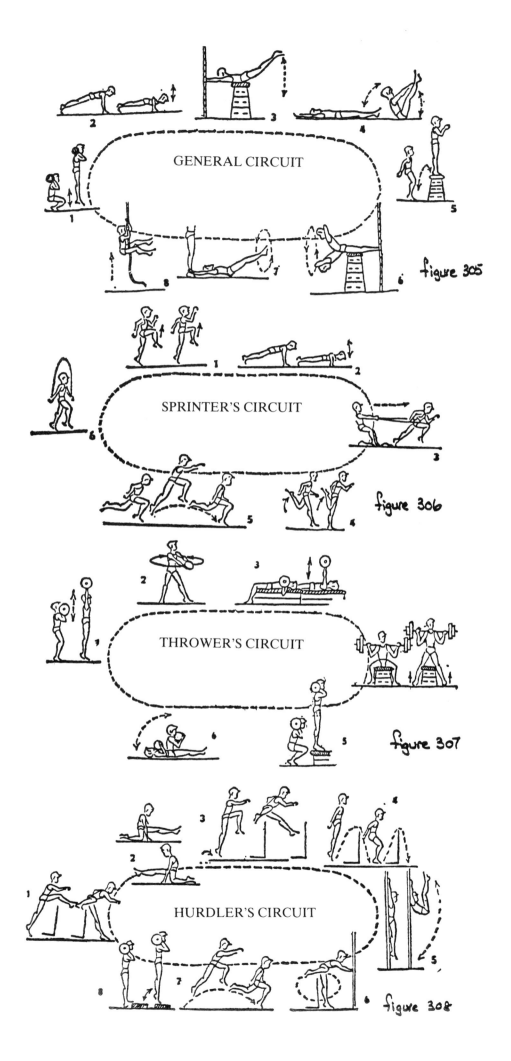

GENERAL CIRCUIT

figure 305

SPRINTER'S CIRCUIT

figure 306

THROWER'S CIRCUIT

figure 307

HURDLER'S CIRCUIT

figure 308

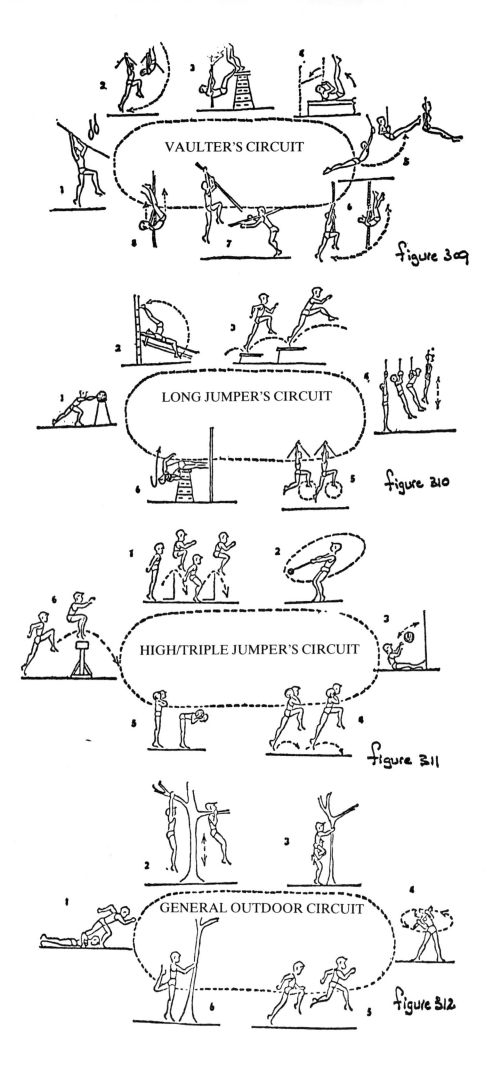

VAULTER'S CIRCUIT

figure 309

LONG JUMPER'S CIRCUIT

figure 310

HIGH/TRIPLE JUMPER'S CIRCUIT

figure 311

GENERAL OUTDOOR CIRCUIT

figure 312

313.   314   315   316

317   318   319   320

321   322   323   324

STRENGTH EXERCISES – TRUNK

325   326   327   328

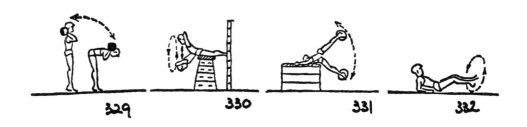

329   330   331   332

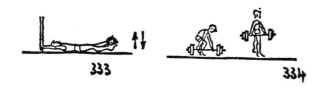

333   334

STRENGTH EXERCISES – LEGS AND HIPS

335

336

337

338

339

340

341

342

343

344

345

STRENGTH EXERCISES – UPPER BODY

346

347

348

349

350

351

352

353

354

355

356

357

358

359

360

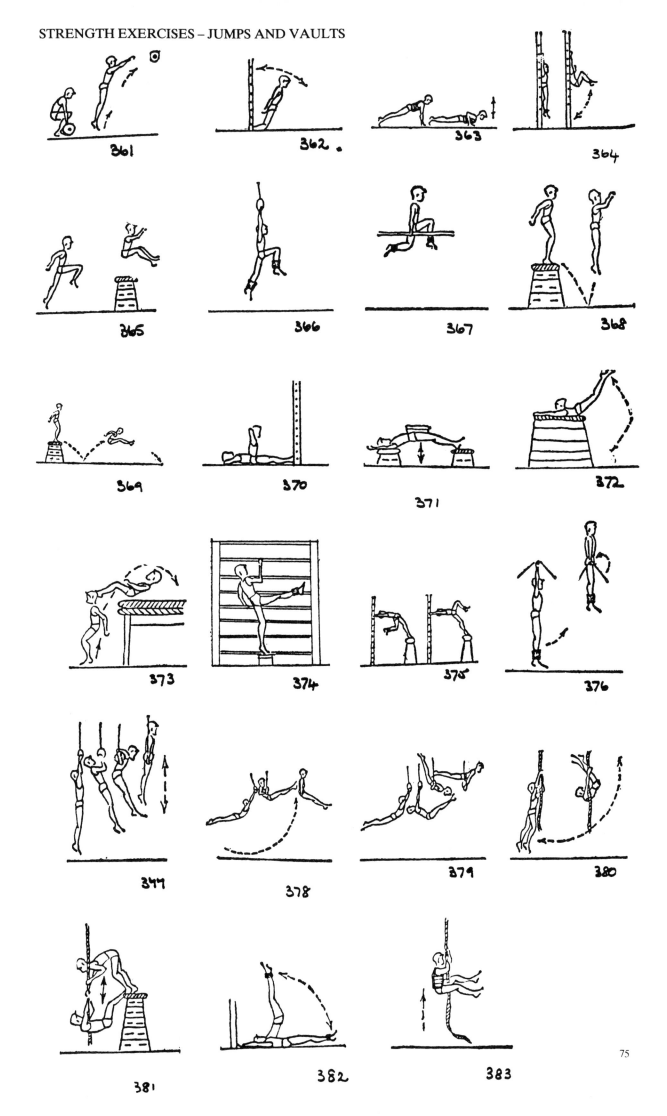

361

362.

363

364

365

366

367

368

369

370

371

372

373

374

375

376

377

378

379

380

381

382

383

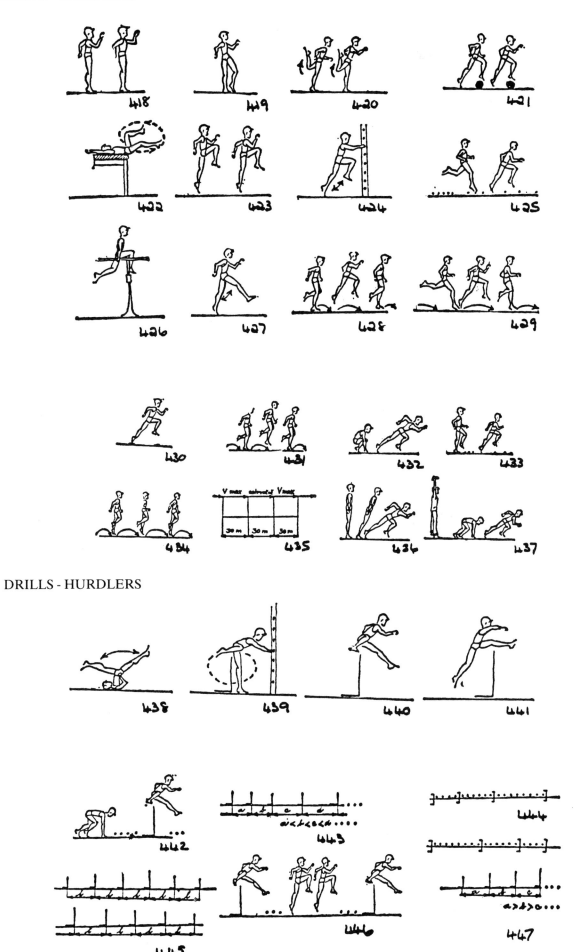

DRILLS - HURDLERS

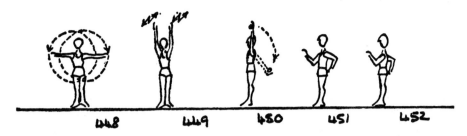

448 449 450 451 452

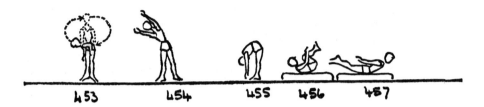

453 454 455 456 457

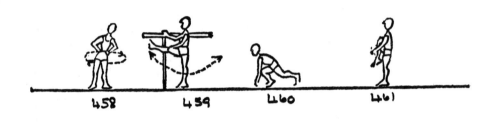

458 459 460 461

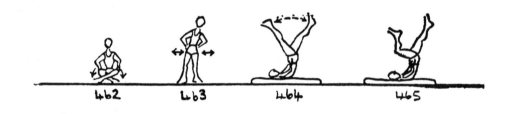

462 463 464 465

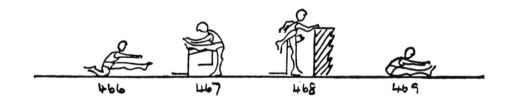

466 467 468 469

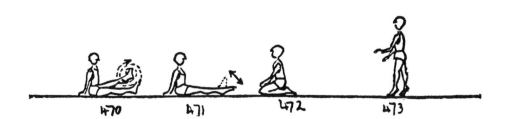

470 471 472 473

figure 474

TRUNK   figure 475

SHOULDERS figure 476

figure 477

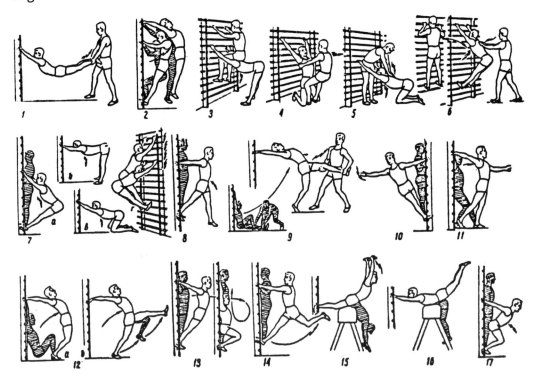

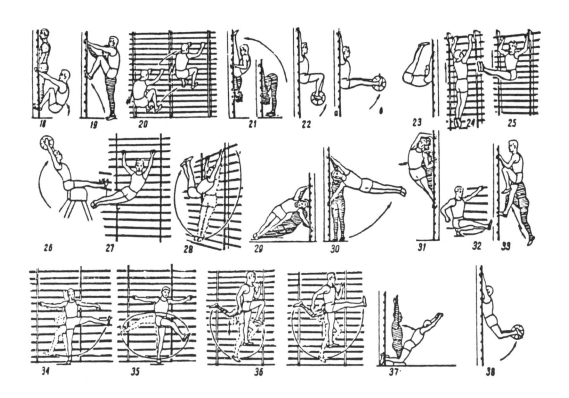

478 479 480 481

482 483 484 485

486 487 488 489

490 491 492 493

494 495 496 497

498 499 500 501

Notes for the Teacher:

The question is often asked "What is the relationship between the work of athletics coaches, and that of Physical Education Teachers?" Broadly speaking, it can be explained as follows:-

Athletics coaching has a service to offer the Physical Education Teacher in his or her work of "educating the child through the physical." This book is an example of part of that service, in that it should be seen as a basic source of reference on technical models and on suggested practices. But what of the Teacher? Can he or she offer a service to the sport? Clearly the answer is yes. The teacher through his or her specialist skills, and using sources of reference such as "But first", can establish the sound technical model that the child must have, if he or she is to embark on a long-term technical and conditioning development, in pursuit of athletic ambition. No less essential than these first technical steps is the positive attitude to, and enthusiasm for, athletics that the good teacher can engender in his or her young charges.

"But first......" was put together in answer to the same question from teachers *and* coaches – "How do I get started?" This last section, specially for the teacher, is again an answer to a question. – "How should I plan my allocation of periods for athletics?" Not every school has the same period allocation, but I hope that the following may provide some ideas on possible rotation of events and on activities for inclusion in lessons:-

Suggested Boys' Programme for Athletics – Year 1 - 3 – To be read in conjunction with Girls' Programme

Year 1

1 Running
   Basic Technique.
   Varied Speed and balance runs.
   Running Games.
   etc.

2 Throwing
   Common Root practices.
   General throws practices.
   Use of sling balls, medicine balls etc.

3 Jumping
   Basic techniques re-
   posture, momentum,
   action of jumping leg.
   General Jumps practices.
   e.g. jumps decathlon etc.

4 Sprint
   Basic Sprinting technique.
   Natural starting technique.
   Speed to be consistent with
   sound technique.
   Repeat runs over 30m – 60m.

5 Shot
   Common root development.
   Basic Putt – 'Early hip'.
   Shift into and thru basic Putt.
   Finish Putt "Tall" and "Square".
   General Throws practice.

Year 2

1 Running
   Basic Technique.
   Varied Speed and balance runs.
   Team runs etc. Paarlauf,
   Continuous relays. Etc.
   Timed runs, etc.

2 Throwing
   Common Root practices.
   General throws practices.
   Varied throwing implements used.
   Introduction of strength
   training practices etc.

3 Jumping
   Basic techniques re –
   posture, momentum,
   action of jumping leg.
   Jumping onto, from, over boxes.
   Flight balance and rotation etc,

4 Sprint
   Basic Sprinting technique.
   Acceleration practices.
   Practices for stride length
   and stride rate.
   Technique to remain sound.
   Repeat runs 30m - 90m etc.

5 Hurdles
   Practices for Hurdle Stride.
   – Lead and trailing legs.
   Runs→ Sprints over heights
   and spacings according to
   individual needs,
   for 3-4-5 strides etc.

Year 3

1 Run – Jump – Throw
   Review of Basics in Jumps,
   Runs, Throws.
   Review fundamentals of
   all events.

2 Run – Jump – Throw

3 Discus – Sprint
   Development practices of
   standing throw and turn throw.
   Block-work. Rolling sprints.
   Bend sprinting. Races.
   Sprint over 40-200m.

4 Long – Hurdles
   Short approach jumps for
   take-off and flight.
   Full approach jumps.
   Rolling hurdles (3-4).
   Broken hurdles.
   Blocks→ 3 hurdles.
   Hurdles Races 60m → 200m.

5 Shot – Middle Distance – Walk
   Development practices of standing
   throw and shift/turn - throw.
   Repetition runs.
   Differential runs. Tactics.
   Walk or run races.

6 High Jump
Straight free leg jump on spot.
Step-in jumps – momentum plus (straight or bent) spring.
3-5 stride take-off for height.
3-7 stride jumps over bar.

7 Hurdles
Running over ditches, using 3-stride, but varying lead leg.
Gradually raise barriers – Lead and trail leg drills.

8 Discus
Common Root development.
Basic Throw – Sling ball – 'Early hip'. Finish tall.
Balanced turns with/without sling ball/discus.
Throws.

9 Long Jump
Balanced run to take-off.
"Stride jump" held flight.
"Jump up" free thigh lift – Punch with arms.
Jump over sand "wall".
7-15 stride approach.

10 Middle Distance
Basic running technique.
Pace judgement runs.
Interval runs – Fartlek – Paarlauf – continuous runs etc.

11 Javelin
Common Root development.
To use med. ball and one-hand weighted ball throws.
3 step throws – early hip.
Finish square and fast.

6 Middle Distance and Walks
Basic running and walking techniques.
Interval runs, Fartlek with hill runs, resistance runs, alternatively paced runs etc.

7 Relays
Starting on visual cues – Baton passing drills – establish check marks.
Races 4 x 100m.
4 x 200m (using visual pass).
Shuttle relays (hurdles) etc.

8 Discus
Standing throw practices using towel in throwing hand to establish basic throw.
Balanced turns into basic throw position.
Full throw with/without turns with discus etc.

9 Shot
Common root revised – basic putt.
Hip lift into throw emphasised putt for height 'Finish Tall'.
Shift into and thru' putt.
Putt with turn etc.

10 Javelin
Standing throw with small weighted ball – then with Javelin.
Throw Javelin along line.
1-5 step throws, elbow under javelin.
Finish square and fast etc.

6 Pole – Relays
Short and full approach for acceleration into take-off.
If fibre pole, work for penetration and bend.
Take over work for Relays.
Baton changes and baton speed races.

7 Javelin – Sprint
Standing → 3 step throws.
Strike from leg - hip - shoulder - arm along javelin.
Acceleration into throw.
Finish square.
Sprint Devt. → races.

8 Triple – Hurdles
3-11 stride approach for technical devt. of "strike".
Hopping and bounding routines. Full approach.
Hurdles Devt. → races.

9 Hammer – Middle Distance
Devt. practices for balance and technique in swings/turns/throw. Hammer used short heavy.
Repetition runs and races.
Introduction to Steeplechase.

10 High – Relays
Short and full approach jumps to develop sound take off.
Rebound jumps; practices with boxes and hurdles.
Relay races and drills.

11 **Discus – Hammer**
Component and full throws practices → regulation implementation. Plus strength training and speed training.

12 **Long - Pole**
Component and full approach jumps plus strength and speed training.

13 **Shot – Javelin**
Component and full throws plus strength and speed training.

14 **Triple – High**
Component and full approach jumps. Plus strength and speed training.

15 **Combined – Events**
Combined Event Competitions for individuals and teams.

---

11 **Hammer**
Swing to throw medicine ball in sack high over shoulder. Turns practised in seated position. Swing, turn, throw with medicine ball etc. Swing, turn, swing, etc.

12 **Long Jump**
Practices for free thigh, arms coordination; straight back; jumping leg.
Action: 1 step - 9 step. *"jump up and out"* – balance in flight. Establish approach accuracy and speed.

13 **Triple Jump**
Revise rhythm of jump (equal phases). Progress distance of each phase. Coordinate arm and free thigh. Use 3-11 stride approach. Establish approach accuracy and speed etc.

14 **High Jump**
Coordinate free leg and arms in 3 step jumps for height – head suspended object. Layout practices. Jumps over elastic bar – emphasise *Height* from take off not lay out.

15 **Pole Vault**
Burkitt exercises → short approach. Vaults with box and bar/elastic. Pole bending practices if fibre glass pole is available. Pull-push phase worked on etc.

16 **Combined Events**
Explanation of Tables and nature of event. Involve athletes in Heptathlon/Decathlon competitions etc.

---

12 **Triple Jump**
Balanced run to take off with "hop" thought of as part of approach. Standing *equal phase*. Triple Jumping on grid balance.

13 **Relays**
Run on visual cue roll ball over line. Passing technique – running out using check on long races. Baton speed must be maintained.

14 **Hammer**
Overhead/over shoulder throws swings – hip countering – to throw – using basketball in sack. Swing, turn, throw. Progress in short hammer.

15 **Pole Vault**
Burkitt exercise, without bar. Then with bar. Carry to plant in sand. Then Burkitt exercise → Box. Hang long – tuck late and fast.

16 **Walks**
Hip swing on spot. Walk down line. Pace judgement races etc.

Notes: applicable to Boys' and Girls' Programmes.

1 Maintain Pattern of a) Warm-up
                        b) Technical work
                        c) Conditioning work
                        d) Warm-down
   Involve competition at c).

2 Use implements, hurdles etc., to suit athletes. *Then* move towards regulation implements etc.

3 Be sure techniques are established before competition is used. Thistle or 5 Star marks may be noted during technical work, but the Award should not take over the lesson!

4 The Thistle or 5 Star Award is a motivational aid and an avenue for expressing technique and *not* an end in itself. Maximum use = 10 -15 mins per lesson if used as an item per-se.

5 Suggested 'teaching area' adapted from asphalt tennis court, with moveable end fence. Sand pit dug at this end, but same apparatus possible at either end.

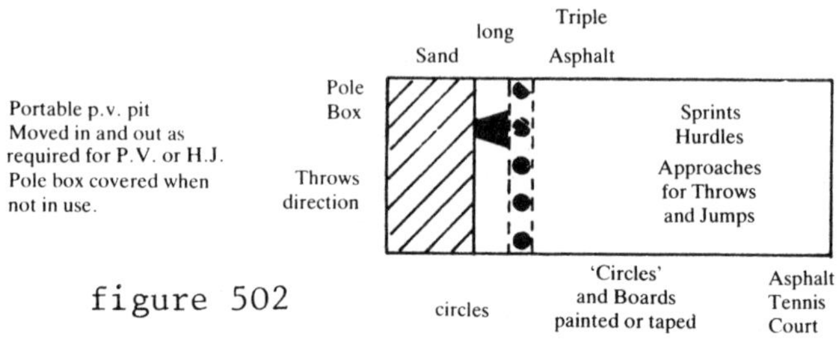

Portable p.v. pit
Moved in and out as
required for P.V. or H.J.
Pole box covered when
not in use.

figure 502

Equipment: 20 - 30 x medicine balls - 0.5kg - 3kg.
      20 - 30 x Stones or shots - 2kg - 5kg.
      20 - 30 x Stones or Discus - 0.5kg - 1.5kg or sling balls.
      20 - 30 x Weighted balls or stones - 1kg
      20 - 30 x Javelins 400 - 800gm
      20 - 30 x Hammers - Varied weight and wire length (or medicine balls in sacks)

Concrete strip 20 - 30 metres to use as 'circles' (2.50m wide) or marks on asphalt.
    8 - 40 x sets blocks
  30 - 60 x hurdles
    4 - 6 x alloy poles
    4 - 6 x fibre poles 12-140 or 14-140.
Kay – Metzeler landing area (pole vault - which may also serve for high jump)
10 - 20 x relay batons
Access to 300m - 400m track.
Long/Triple pit.
High Jump/Pole Vault Stands and Fibre glass Bars. Elastic "bar" for teaching.

6 Safety procedures and rules of competition are assumed to be included in lessons where appropriate.

Suggested Girls' Programme for Athletics — Year 1 - 3 — To be read in conjunction with Boys' Programme

	Year 1	Year 2	Year 3
1	Running	Running	Run - Jump - Throw
2	Throwing	Throwing	Run - Jump - Throw
3	Jumping	Jumping	Discus - Sprint
4	Sprint	Sprint	Long - Hurdles
5	Shot	Hurdles	Shot - Middle Distance
6	High	Middle Distance	High - Relays
7	Hurdles	Relays	Javelin - Walk
8	Discus	Discus	Combined Events
9	Long	Shot	
10	Middle Distance	Javelin	
11	Javelin	Long	
12	Relays	High	

Notes: Applicable to Boys and Girls Programmes.

1 Content should be as per same disciplines for boys.

2 The 'pairing' of disciplines is based on variety and distribution of emphasis rather than on proven parity etc.

3 The order of introducing disciplines has been based on the following:-
  Girls Year 1: 1-3 - As for Year 1
                  4-9 - Run-Throw-Jump/repeated.
                  10-12 - The remaining disciplines.

Emphasis is on ensuring concentrated teaching in years 1 and 2 – then gentle development in year 3.

Girls Year 2: 1-3 As for Year 1
                 4-12 All track: All throws: All Jumps
Girls Year 3: 1 2 reviewing basics.
                 3-7 review and develop each discipline.
                 Walks + 8 - intro. these disciplines
Boys Year 1: 1-3 - As for Girls
                 4-15 - Run-Throw-Jump/repeated.
                 16 - Intro. Walks

Boys Year 2: 1-3 - As for Girls
4-15 - All Track: All Throws: All Jumps.
16 - Intro. Multi-Event disciplines.
Boys Year 3: 1-2 - Reviewing Basics
3-14 - Review and Develop each discipline.
(Intro. Steeplechase) -
2 x ½ session per discipline
15 - Review Multi-Event discipline.

4 By the end of Year 2, *most* athletes will have shown their aptitude for one or several disciplines. Consequently there is a case for group work "by interest" in year 3. However, Year 3 offers a "last chance" to help the athlete decide on his/her better discipline. Bear in mind the late developer should have been given a thorough grounding of sound techniques to be applied more effectively when he/she 'matures'.

5 *Participation* with sound technique is good.
Competition with bad technique is bad even if success → enjoyment → greater desire for participation.
Thistle Award/or 5 Star Award is very valuable as an avenue for *participation* and a personal testing medium, but must not be abused.
Direct Technical Development at this phase and performance/competition Development when technique is sound.
This is a most exacting test of teaching ability - but, in the long term is of immeasurable benefit to athlete, school and sport.

6 Make learning enjoyable – please!
We need to keep happy athletes in our sport.

Some Suggestions for Athletes – Related Activities

1 Continuous Relay:

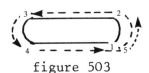

figure 503

E.g. 400m Track - 5 man teams - (1, 2, 3, 4, 5) - Nos. 1 and 5 stand at start/finish; No. 2 stands at 100m; No. 3 at 200m; No. 4 at 300m. No. 1 runs to 100m - hands over to No. 2 and remains at 100 - while No. 2 runs to 200m etc.
Select balanced teams and aim to keep laps at a target time - say 64 secs. per lap. (16 secs. per 100m). Each team has 10 points to start with, and loses a point if team is 2 secs. faster or slower than the target time.
Run for 20 mins. - then progress → 60 mins. from session to session.
Last 2 mins. of each session is a race: 3 points to 1st; 2 points to 2nd, 1 point to 3rd - i.e. winning team = 13 points maximum.

2 Paarlauf:

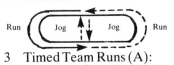

figure 504

As continuous relay, but 2 men teams. Normally it means that each athlete runs 200m - and jogs across infield during "recovery". It is easiest organized by having the change overs midway down each straight - this keeps the jog "recovery" to the shortest distance.

3 Timed Team Runs (A):

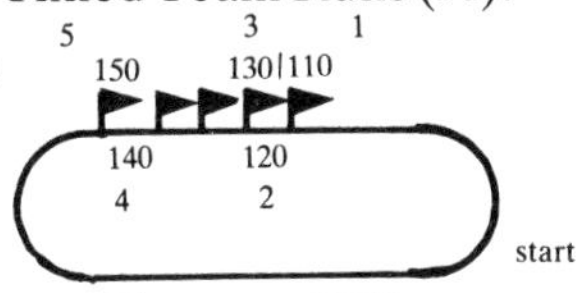

figure 505

E.g. decide a 'time' - say 20 secs. of running - with 2 mins. rest between runs. Place flags or markers 150m, 140m, 130m, 120m, and 110m from starting point. Balanced teams are selected. Blow whistle to start and after 20 secs. Athlete scores 1 point for every flag/marker he passes.
Average score of each team is used to decide "winners". This may be arranged to produce 2 - 3 sets of 3 - 5 runs. (10 mins between sets). This should help assess basis of times, No. of repetitions and intervals for 150's. (Captain of team collects scores).

4 Timed Team Runs (B):

Similar to (3) - Athletes *all* run 150m - but athlete scores 5 points for 20 secs; 4 points = 21.5; 3 points = 23.0; 2 points = 24.5; 1 point = 26.0. Scores averaged again.

5 Time Trials:

These may be arranged over orthodox distances, but tests may also be performed over approx. distances - say round a park or wood, etc. (Aerobic/endurance test). - or a standardised distance for evaluation purposes on a test-retest situation - e.g. 40m - (speed) - 3rd hurdle touch down (speed technique) etc.

6 Fartlek:

"Playing with distance and speed". This is best done in attractive changing terrain, e.g. woodland, seaside.
E.g. - 5 mins. easy jog → 5 mins. of 10 sec. stride, 20 sec. jog → 2 mins. jog → 5 mins. of sprint 5 - 10 sec. jog 20 - 25 sec. → 2 mins. jog → 2 mins. of 5 sec. high knees - 25 sec. jog → 5 mins. of hill runs - (jog back recovery) (say 10 x 50m hills → 2 mins. jog → 10 mins. stretching, bounding, etc. → 5 mins. jog to finish. "As you like it".

7 Throws Football:

Teams line up on a football field. A sling-ball is used and technique agreed upon. i.e. Javelin; Discus; Hammer. 'Ball' is thrown from where it lands - 'Goals' scored by putting 'Ball' over opponents line. A medicine ball and chest passes (basic basketball style) may be used as a shot put equivalent.

8	Team Jumps Decathlon:	Using the jumps decathlon tables - teams scores are averaged. Ensure balanced teams - 3 - 6 attempts per event.
9	Pole-Vault - Distance:	Athlete plants pole in sand and object is to vault *along* the long jump pit - for distance. (This helps encourage 'swing' phase).
10	'Heading' for Height:	Athlete jumps to head a suspended object from a short approach → full approach. Object is raised by having it suspended from something like a beam. (This develops Take- off Technique).
11	Team Multi-Event:	Teams are balanced to allow each athlete to perform 2 or more events of his choice. Peformance in each event is scored against points tables (e.g. Thistle/5 Star). Team points are averaged. Competition is based on set events - e.g. decathlon events, heptathlon events. Other events may also be considered.
12	Odd-Throws:	Special exercises may be used as competition 'Events' e.g. Standing overhead throw - backward/forward caber - toss - Scottish style. Weight-throw for height Caber throw (log approx. 1 - 2 metres long) - 1 hand - supporting leg with other hand. Discus throw with small shot.
13	Multiple Hurdles:	Say 4 hurdles spaced for 5 - 6 strides + approach and run-off. A further 4 hurdles are set-up beside these, but in opposite direction. Object - run over 100 hurdles. Keeping technique sound despite progressive fatigue.
14	Inter-Club/Team Field Events Contest:	Each team/club supplies A & B string for field events. A + B performances are aggregated for each event, and points are awarded as, say, 10 pts. for 1st team, 9 for 2nd, 8 for 3rd etc. - total points are added together for all events and team with largest no. of points wins.
15	Relays Meet:	Teams are picked for a selected number of relays events. Points are scored for teams as they finish in the final e.g. 6 pts. 1st., 5 pts. 2nd. etc. Winning team scores most points. 4 x 100; 4 x 400; 4 x 4 laps Steeplechase; Swedish Medley: 400-300-200-100 4 x 200; 4 x 800; 4 x 100m Hurdles (shuttle). Medley: 400-200, 200-800 etc.
16	Cross-Country Relay:	– Straight forward x 1 lap circuit - or each athlete running separate stretch
17	"Play" Conditioning:	– Obstacle races onto, over, from boxes and benches. – Piggy-back races. – Rope-Swing "Vaults". – Medicine Ball Tennis (Volley-Ball net). – Standing High Jumps. – Soccer - Throw-in for Distance. – Sling-Ball/Medicine Ball/Stone/Log/etc. Throws - "Slinging", "Pushing", "Heaving", "Overhead-Striking" etc. – Etc.
18	"Beat the Clock":	Athlete runs as far as he can for 15 sec. and marks distance achieved. He repeats this at 3 minute intervals, over 30 secs, 45 secs, 60 secs, then attempts to beat these distances on the way down: 60 secs, 45 secs, 30 secs, and 15 secs.
19	Handicap Races:	To aid motivation and ensure progression of speed training. In Sprints, the athletes race over - say 60m, with 1 - 10 metre starts according to ability. In endurance runs - say in the country or on roads - Handicaps are again according to ability - but on the basis of "Time Starts" e.g. 30 secs → 5 mins etc.
20	Resistance Runs:	E.g. Hills (Long = 100m - 200m) (Short = 30m - 60m): Sand Dunes; Harness Runs (Tyre & Rope harness); Surf running; with weighted jacket; etc.
21	Special Runs:	Bounding; Hopping; High Knees; Running & Twisting shoulders from side to side; skipping - sideways, for height etc.; running on heels; running in half-squat (Groucho Marx runs); etc.

SAFETY

A Introduction

Although without the same propensity towards traumatic injury as such sports as soccer, rugby, skiing or boxing, athletics nevertheless does present situations from which injury can result. Knowledge of these, and how to avoid them, is an important part of the coach's skill.

B Classification

The types of injury which result can be divided into two main categories:-

(a)   Self inflicted

(b)   Externally inflicted

C Self inflicted injuries

Such injuries mostly involve damage to the soft tissue, such as muscle or tendon tears, sprains, strains or deep bruising. They mainly result from over-stress in training or competition.

Wear and tear injuries of the bony structure, particularly at joints, are quite common among athletes. Stress fractures (small hair-like splits which run along the length of the bone) are a particular hazard for distance runners.

All such injuries respond well to *prompt* initial reduction of the training load.

D Externally inflicted

This group of injuries is important not only because of the resultant loss of vital training time, and thereby reduction in competitive capacity, but because they carry a risk to the perpetrator (or the organising agent, be it school, club or association) which makes them liable to prosecution in law. Most competitors are covered by compulsory insurance taken out by the meeting promoter, but not all training venues or situations are similarly covered. Check that *your* club is covered, or failing that see that *you* are. Policies such as golfers policies are available at reasonable rates.

The responsibility for avoiding this type of injury rests with all involved—see the A.A.A. pamphlet 'Safety Measures in Athletics' reproduced at the end of this chapter. Many general and specific recommendations are made concerning the organisation and conduct of training and competition. It should be read *carefully* by *all* coaches. In addition the following general guidelines will be found useful:-

1. Running events

1.i. **At the Track:-**

(a) Instil good lane discipline into your charges;

    warm up only in the outer lanes

    observe local 'fast lane' arrangements

    don't hold 'conferences' on the track

    be always considerate of the needs of other track users

(b) Be conscious that grass and synthetic surfaces become slippery in wet conditions. Caution should be exercised in the management of hurdles and high jump training in particular.

(c) The infield is generally the *only* provision for throws training. Even if it is not used for such at your own track, you are teaching dangerous habits if you permit your athletes to cross it in an undisciplined manner. These habits can lead to fatalities when they go to tracks where throwers commonly use the infield. Safety in these areas is the repsonsibility of thrower *and* runners, *and* their coaches alike. Don't be negligent in this respect.

1.ii. **Running away from the Track**

(a) Roads are made for the use of vehicles; therefore runners should avoid running on them where possible. Where there are footpaths runners should be encouraged to use them, unless they are frequently interrupted by road intersections or by their worn state or/plus fatigue makes foot and ankle injuries a probability.

(b) Roads are *hard* surfaces which increases the likelihood of stress problems. Keep a careful check on your athletes when high mileages and speed work is programmed.

(c) Athletes should run *facing the oncoming traffic, even when running on pavements.*

(d) Runners *should be seen* - especialy at night by wearing light, bright or reflective clothing. Even in daylight with a low, bright sun from behind, the driver's vision is often impaired.

1.iii **Hurdling**

(a) In addition to the guidelines set out in 'Safety Measures', care should be taken to see that improvised equipment of the types used particularly with novices is reasonably safe.

(b) The ends of canes can damage eyes if not protected by a cork or some similiar device.

(c) Elasticated hurdle bars are capable of catapulting the hurdle some distance if hit hard by the athlete.

(d) Hurdles should be greased and top bars should be secure.

(e) They should be correctly placed relative to their use with the counter-balance weights also relatively correctly positioned.

(f) Hurdles should NEVER ber crossed in the wrong direction (i.e. *from* the landing side).

Field Events

Further to 'Safety Measures', the coach should note the following:-

(a) all landing areas should preferably be covered by a proper cover sheet.

(b) Their size and density should be adequate for the use to which they are being put (i.e. heavier jumpers and those landing from greater heights require thickest protection, whilst those of inconsistent or long flight parabolas require greatest area).

(c) The position of take-off in high jump determines the point of landing. It should be close to the nearer upright.

(d) Elastic crossbars used in training lessen the risk of injury and improve confidence.

(e) Triangular crossbars are dangerous for 'floppers'.

(f) Fibre-glass vaulting poles break if misused, therefore always:-

protect the distant end with a proper pole 'bung'.

hold it correctly, i.e. with the outside of its natural bend top-left (at 11 o'clock or 300°) in the plant position.

avoid dropping it (arrange for people to catch it after the vault).

don't leave it lying about outside its tube for people to step on.'

always use a pole of the *correct* strength, according to the weight of athlete using it and the amount of force that he can put into it. A pole bending more than 90° is being overstressed.

don't use a fibre-glass pole where there is an old fashioned box with a vertical back.

(g) **In horizontal jumps see that:-**

no-jump indicator board recesses are safely blocked out.

athletes' footwear and protection are adequate.

platforms for skill work are large enough and strong enough for their purpose.

other athletes do not encroach onto the runway when in use.

(h) **Throwing events**

The safety rules when throwing is in progress are:-
1. NEVER throw towards anyone - therefore the thrower MUST look to ensure that the landing area is clear BEFORE throwing.
2. NEVER collect the implement until ALL have thrown, then collect together.
3. NEVER stand in front of the thrower.
4. NEVER run with a javelin, nor run to collect it.
5. ALWAYS push the javelin into a vertical position, then pull it vertically from the ground.
6. ALWAYS carry javelins vertically, point down in front of you.

Coaches should additionally ensure that implements are well maintained and stored (particular care needs to be taken to see that hammers are hung on hooks and that spindles are kept free and oiled). Ensure also that the surfaces and rims of throwing circles are safe.

WHERE POSSIBLE THROWING AREAS SHOULD BE ROPED OFF SO THAT OTHERS CANNOT ENCROACH.

3. IN THE WEIGHT ROOM

The weight room is not the place for practical jokers and fooling about. It is the coach's duty to teach his athletes respect for its inherent dangers.

Simple rules to ensure safety are:-
1. Always *lift in groups of* at least *three,* two of whom act as 'spotters'.
2. Always ensure that the bar is *correctly loaded* and *collars are tightened.*
3. Always lift *within* one's ability until *absolutely* competent as a lifter.

In some lifts where the bar is taken from the ground, novice lifters using light loads (e.g. below 60kgs/132lbs) endanger their backs by having to lift from too low a starting position. This can be corrected by raising the bar onto blocks or by making wooden discs of 50cm diameter.

Initial loadings can be estimated by the coach (according to the size, age, experience of the athlete). *Err on the light side* and be present at the first attempts. Adjust them according to the reaction of the athlete.

'Multigyms' or 'Polygyms' are IDEAL and safe pieces of strength trainig equipment for novice lifters and those doing light load/high repetition schedules. Use them where available.

The key points of SAFE form in lifting are shown in figure 506.

Figure 506 Good form in weightlifting
(a) Feet firmly on floor
(b) Shins close to bar
(c) Flat back
(d) Head up
(e) Pull vertically
(f) Stop bar on thighs when lowering

4. IN THE GYMNASIUM

When using gym facilities pay attention to:-

   (i) the possibility of injury as the result of running into walls (i.e. always allow 'slowing down space' in running activities). Organise 'shuttle relays' around markers set *away* from the walls.

   (ii) the clear demarkation of working areas where there is some danger element in the activities (e.g. indoor shot or slingball). Gym benches can be gainfully used for this purpose.

   (iii) the safety and suitability of apparatus and provide adequate protection in case of falls by using gym mats.

When using hopping and bounding exercises indoors see that landing surfaces, particularly *hard* floors, are well cushioned to prevent jarring and stress injuries. Gym mats, liberally used, will suffice.

The good coach will find challenging and interesting ways to present this work to groups of young athletes. He will emphasise the rhythmic, or skill element, and supplement this by team, partial team, and individual competition to construct a varied, purposeful, and enjoyable programme.

5. WHAT TO DO WHEN INJURY OCCURS

It is difficult to give detailed advice without getting into contestable areas of medical opinion and etiquette.

In the common instances of pulls, strains and bruising, the coach should try to reduce the amount of internal bleeding by:-

     I - mmobilising the limb
     (or at least reducing use of it)
     C - ompression bandage
     E - levate

These steps reduce blood flow and thereby hasten recovery time.

The application of cold compresses or ice packs can be of help. If the latter are kept stationary or applied without sufficient protection between the ice and skin then skin damage can be caused.

Having done that SEEK EXPERT MEDICAL HELP OR ADVICE QUICKLY.

In instances of very serious injury e.g. from throwing implement or vehicles then:-
1. Telephone for doctor or ambulance immediately.
2. Take steps to arrest any serious bleeding.
3. Unless ABSOLUTELY certain that there is no skeletal or internal damage place in foetal position (lying on side with legs slightly tucked).
4. Keep warm and dry until experienced help arrives.
5. Ensure that the airway is kept CLEAR.

6. REFERENCES FOR FURTHER READING

All advice concerning safe procedures is enshrined in the former A.A.A. leaflet 'Safety Measures in Athletics' (see next page) and in the Rule Book.

Publications about the treatment of sports injuries do exist but we hesitate to direct the coach towards them. A little knowledge can be a very dangerous thing. Those wishing to know more are advised to begin by taking a St. John's or St. Andrew's Ambulance Course.

SAFETY MEASURES IN ATHLETICS

(A leaflet issued by the former Amateur Athletic Association)

These recommendations should be regarded as guide lines for teachers, coaches and participants. They should be implemented or amended to suit local conditions, the aim being, to ensure safety at all times.

The Young Athletes Committee recommends that athletics be regarded as a sport for all ages.

There is wide participation by young children and it should be the aim of all teachers and coaches to hold this interest through out the school and club career up to adult age through the organisation of competition and training which permits wide participation by competitors of different abilities.

RESPONSIBILITY

Athletics is a sport in which a variety of running, jumping and throwing activities may be taking place at the same time. Very often in training and competition athletes are acting under comsiderable stress. It is essential therefore, to maintain a constant awareness of their inherent dangers, and to plan facilities and practices with this in mind.

The responsibility for safety rests with everyone concerned in the development of the sport; the officials who plan the initial layout of facilities, the owners and groundsmen responsible for maintaining these efficiently, the teacher and club coach responsible for the supervision of training, and the officials responsible for the organisation of competitions at all levels. Finally the athlete himself is equally responsible.

THE PREPARATION AND PROGRESSION OF TRAINING

The teacher or coach should ensure that each new activity and each stage of a new activity is carefully introduced so that the young athlete is made fully aware of the potential dangers involved, of the necessary safety precautions to be observed and of the rules which must be obeyed. A special obligation rests on the teacher, coach and participant to see that these precautions are carried out during training. It is unwise to hurry these preliminary stages. Sufficient time should be given to the early stages of training so that safe habits are formed from the outset.

CONTROL

In the teaching of athletics much depends on the teacher-pupil relationship and on the development of self discipline in all members of the class, club or group. It is only when the teacher or coach has established such trust that activities with an element of danger may be attempted.

Extra vigilance is necessary at training sessions or during competition where the teacher, coach or pupils are assisting with the recording of standards (judging, measuring, timekeeping, photographing, etc.). Spectators should remain behind the barrier or watch from a safe distance. They should never crowd around the track or field event areas.

FIELD EVENTS

Although field events, especially throwing events, can be dangerous unless they are conducted and supervised with care, their suitability as a worthwhile athletic activity for young people is borne out by the hundreds of thousands of throws and jumps that are made each year without mishap.

The Schools' Consultative Committee suggests the following measures that can reasonably be applied to ensure safety in most circumstances.

THROWING

(a) GENERAL

1. Equipment should be kept in good repair and stored in a safe place.
2. Throwing implements should at all times be treated with respect. They should not be played about with or mishandled, especially when being carried from the pavilion or school to the playing field or track.
3. There should be adequate supervision at distribution and the apparatus should be transported in a safe manner. Nets or baskets can be of help when apparatus is carried in bulk.
4. Initially, training should be undertaken under the control of the teacher or coach. They, through experience and good judgement, will decide if and when athletes are capable of assuming responsibility themselves and can be permitted to undertake practices on their own.
5. All throwers should stand well behind the appropriate circle or scratch line and remain there until the appropriate time to make a throw.
6. The thrower himself should make sure that there is no one in the landing area or probable line of flight of the implement before the throw is made.
   IT IS VERY IMPORTANT THAT THIS RESPONSIBILITY SHOUD REST WITH THE THROWER AS WELL AS WITH THE TEACHER OR COACH OR OFFICIAL.
7. After throwing, the thrower should remain behind the circle or scratch line and must not immediately retrieve the implement. It should be retrieved only on instruction when all members of the group have thrown. Under no circumstances should a javelin, discus, shot or hammer be thrown back to the scratch line or throwing circle.
8. Wet implements increase the chances of accidents and extra vigilance should be exercised in such conditions, taking particular care to allow for implements sliding after landing.
9. In wet conditions grass and some artificial surfaces can prove slippery and dangerous. Particular care should then be exercised to ensure that runways and take off areas are suitable for use.

(b) JAVELIN

1. Both ends of javelins are dangerous. Special care should therefore be taken in controlling their use.
2. They should never be permitted to remain stuck in the ground at an angle.
3. Special care should be taken to establish a safe and controlled routine in retrieving the javelins.

(c) DISCUS

Being a rotational event, greater space is required between participants in class or group practices. The areas of greatest danger are to the right of a right handed thrower and to the left of a left handed thrower.

(d) HAMMER

1. The hammer event should be conducted only in a strictly controlled situation.
2. Since it is more difficult to predict the probable direction of flight, greater care should be taken in the siting of practice venues and in coaching.
3. Cages are strongly recommended for hammmer throwing in competition. They are essential when other events are taking place within throwing range and are mandatory where events are held under A.A.A. rules.
4. Whenever possible cages should also be provided for practice and coaching. However, where conditions and facilities are favourable, it is possible for experienced and well qualified coaches to undertake training in open spaces under controlled conditions provided that a safe area of the playing field or training area can be specially set apart.
5. The coach and any other members of the group should stand well back to the side of the circle where the path of the hammer is at its lowest point.
6. They should always watch the implement when a throw is actually being made.

JUMPS – GENERAL

1. Wood or concrete edges to the pits should be flush with the surrounding ground.
2. Any hard surfaces should be protected to ensure soft landings.
3. The sand used in all pits should be sharp sand and deep enough to prevent jarring on landing.
4. Pits should be dug before use and also at frequent intervals during use.
5. It is important to ensure that all run up areas are well maintained, especially at take off points.
6. Athletes, teachers, coaches and officials should take particular care to ensure that no jump is made while the pit is being dug or raked and that spades, forks and rakes are not left where they can cause injury.

VERTICAL JUMPS

1. For younger pupils, beginners and preliminary practices the sand pit landing area for high jumps can be used quite safely for training purposes at low heights.
2. In those styles of jumping in which the jumper normally lands on his feet (i.e. Scissors, Western Roll and Cut Off styles of High Jumping, and Pole Vaulting using metal poles) sand provides a safe and acceptable landing area.
3. For those styles of jumping in which it is normal for the athlete to land on his back (i.e. Fosbury and Straddle style of high Jumping, and Pole Vaulting with fiberglass poles) commercially manufactured foam landing areas are recommended.
4. Minimum recommended sizes for competition are:
   (a) Pole Vault – 5mx 5m square excluding front protection pads.
   (b) High Jump – Min. 5m x 4m. In schools competition the suitable size is 5m x 2.5m.
5. Larger landing areas for vertical jumps provide safer conditions.
6. Smaller landing areas for high jump are acceptable for training when the point of take off can be established with reasonable certainty and the teacher or coach is qualified and experienced in the event.

7. individual units should be fastened together to reduce the risk of athletes going through the joins between two sections.

8. All foam landing areas should be capable of preventing the athlete from bottoming. Good manufacturers will give specific guarantees in this respect.

9. Soft landing areas deteriorate. They should be regularly inspected and maintained.

HIGH JUMP

1. Unless spikes are worn, grass and some artificial surfaces are not very suitable for take off areas.

2. Bars of circular section are more suitable for "Fosbury Flop" style of jumping.

HORIZONTAL JUMPS

1. Take off boards should be firmly fixed flush with the surface of the runway and so positioned that there is no danger of the jumper landing on the pit surround.

2. Where possible, it is advantageous to provide separate facilities for long jump and triple jump.

3. Where it is possible to provide only a single landing area it is better to make this wider than usual so that adjacent runways can be provided.

POLE VAULT

1. Wooden or concrete surrounds and hard surfaces at the front of built up landing areas are dangerous.

2. Planting boxes should be kept in good repair. Vertical back plates are only suitable for rigid poles. Back plates should slope away from the direction of run up to allow for the bending of fiber glass-poles

TRACK EVENTS

Of their nature track events present few safety problems.

1. Careful instruction should be given at the earliest opportunity to prevent accidents from spikes.

2. In events of more than one lap, in which all or part of the race is not run in lanes, due consideration should be given to the number of athletes who are permitted to contest any one race in order to avoid accidents arising from jostling for position.

3. Hurdles should be well maintained and care should be taken to ensure precautions for safety when improvised hurdles are used for practice.

4. Hurdles should only be used in the correct direction.

5. Steeplechase barriers should be stable, well maintained and conform to A.A.A. regulations. Especially this is so for the water jump landing area.

6. In wet conditions, grass and some artificial surfaces are not suitable for hurdling unless suitable footwear is worn.

CROSS COUNTRY

1. The safety of competitors should be of paramount importance when planning the course.

2. The start should be sufficiently wide to eliminate any danger of spiking. There should be a clear, wide and lengthy run before any narrowing of the course to prevent bunching up and queuing of competitors.

3. Basic provision should include first aid and casualty transport, washing and changing facilities and drinks to counter the effects of adverse weather conditions.

CARE IN THE USE OF STARTING PISTOLS

1. There is no such thing as a safe fire-arm. Large bore starting pistols and those capable of conversion to take live ammunition are subject to licence, regular police notification and strict safety precautions.

2. A starting pistol should never be held close to the face.

3. Ammunition should never be tampered with.

4. A starting pistol should never be left loaded.

5. For security reasons starting pistols should be locked in a safe place after use.

6. The loss of guns and ammunition should be investigated immediately and if necessary reported.

INSURANCE COVER OF ATHLETICS MEETINGS

1. Local associations and organisers of school, youth and club events, should check their existing policies and also those arranged through the Local Education Authority. They are strongly advised to ensure that proper indemnity, personal accident and public liability insurance cover has been arranged.

2. Special consideration should be given to ensuring that approved adults, parent and voluntary helpers are covered as well as the approved officials and teachers.

3. Where organisers of athletic events are not sure that the existing policies provide sufficient insurance cover, they are strongly advised to make separate and additional cover through agencies or through the special arrangements of the English Schools A.A., Welsh Schools A.A. or the Amateur Athletic Association.

NOTES